THE GITA AND THE QURAN

By
PANDIT SUNDERLAL

Rendered into English

By

SYED ASADULLAH

PILGRIMS

PILGRIMS PUBLISHING
◆ Varanasi ◆

THE GITA AND THE QURAN

Pandit Sunderlal

Published by:
PILGRIMS PUBLISHING

An imprint of:
PILGRIMS BOOK HOUSE
(Distributors in India)
B 27/98 A-8, Nawabganj Road
Durga Kund, Varanasi-221010, India
Tel: 91-542- 2314060,
Fax: 91-542- 2312456
E-mail: pilgrims@satyam.net.in
Website: www.pilgrimsbooks.com

Cover Design by Asha Mishra

ISBN: 81-7769-333-6

Printed in India at Pilgrim Press Pvt. Ltd. Lalpur Varanasi

PREFACE

The Bhagavad Gita is the most well known book from the Indian epic, the Mahabharata. The Qur'an (Koran) is the book of Islam, the word of God, the book, which guides the followers of Islam.

The first part of the book outlines the similarities between the two faiths. It concentrates on the common themes. Throughout the text we are enlightened by verses from the various holy writings.

Many great saints, sages, teachers and writers have sought to interpret the themes encompassing the two faiths; Kabir and the Sufi poet, Maulana Rumi, are two of the more famous. Guru Nanak, the founder of Sikhism, looked for a path between the two great religions of the Hindu and the Muslim. He defined a new order, yet this too adhered to the central themes of the two faiths.

A quote from Kabir concerns the disunity of humanity and its adherence to useless dogma. *"The entire world is labouring under a great harmful delusion. One swears by the Veda the other by the Qur'an. One speaks of hell, another of heaven. There really is no difference between the two paths."*

In the second half of the book the author considers in more depth the basic tenets of the two religious texts. In particular he has chosen verses from the Qur'an that attempt to give the reader a clearer grasp of why Islam is misunderstood. Of course throughout its history there have been those who have sought to reinterpret the Qur'an for their own agendas. This translation helps us to choose for ourselves how the words should be interpreted.

The Gita and the Qur'an is an interesting example of a book, which examines the interrelationship of differing faiths. Written by Pandit Sunderlal and translated by Syed Asadullah, it offers us a side-by-side comparison of Hinduism and Islam. In all religion basic themes of humanity are to the fore, themes, which should unite the world's people and not divide them.

Bob Gibbons
Siân Pritchard-Jones
Kathmandu 2004

CONTENTS

FOREWORD

When in 1955 an association of scholars was formed in Hyderabad under the name of the "Institute of Indo-Middle East Cultural Studies" with the object of "advancing and strengthening cultural understanding between India and the countries of the Middle East by promoting a wider knowledge and appreciation of their arts and literatures," the initial programme chalked out by the Institute necessarily visualized, among other items, a process of acquainting, as a preliminary requisite, the people of one region with the bases on which rested the cultural edifice of the people of the other region. In the pursuit of this initial task, it was realized that, in as much as the two cultures were rooted in religion, at least a bird's eye view of their respective bases should be presented by way of interpreting one to the other, and of supplying the necessary background to the appreciation of the cultural problems which may face the two regions from time to time. In the series of works undertaken under this particular item, the rendering into English of Pandit Sunderlal's *Gītā Aur Qur'ān* forms the opening number, to be followed shortly by other publications now in the press, including "An Outline of the Cultural History of India" each chapter of which has been contributed by a scholar competent to deal with the subject falling under it.

In this small work, "The Gītā and the Qur'ān," the author has epitomized the essential teachings of the Gītā on the one hand, and of the Qur'ān on the other, and attempted to show how closely they resemble each other in their basic teachings. People of understanding everywhere will see therein a noble attempt made by a high-minded godly man to forge happy relations between one cultural unit and another, and point the way to an universal outlook on life among mankind. Should scholars of the type of Pandit Sunderlal belonging to different religious denominations undertake to disclose to the world at large from out of their own cultural heritage what is great in each and of universal import, and aim at amity between one culture and another, we may yet hope to develop mankind into one people and one world.

I am thankful to Pandit Sunderlal for the readiness with which he was pleased to allow the Institute to render his beautiful work into English, and Mr. Syed Asadullah, an associate member of the Institute, for having given us an easily intelligible rendering of it into English. My thanks are also due to Dr. Aryendra Sarma, Professor of Sanskrit, Osmania University, for having transliterated the Sanskrit terms employed in the work, and to Mr. N. C. S.

Venkatachari of the Ajanta Publications, Secunderabad, for having read the proofs while the work was in the press.

In conclusion, I deem it my duty to place on record the Institute's sense of thankfulness to Mawlana Abul Kalam Azad, Education Minister of India, Dr. Syed Mahmud, Minister in the Ministry of External Affairs, Government of India, and Dr. B. Rama Krishna Rao, at Present Governor of Kerala, for the scholarly interest which they have evinced in the work of the Institute, and to the Government of India in the Ministry of Education for having afforded generous financial aid to the Institute to begin in time its initial programme as originally planned.

HYDERABAD-DN., **SYED ABDUL LATIF,**
Feb. 1, 1957 *President.*

TRANSLATOR'S NOTE

In rendering into English *Gītā aur Qur'ān* of Pandit Sunderlal of Delhi, my primary aim was to reproduce, as far as was possible for me, the thought-content of the original. My task was greatly lightened by the valuable suggestions offered to me from time to time by Dr. Syed Abdul Latif, President of the Institute of Indo-Middle East Cultural Studies, and by the opportunity of revision of various passages effected under his sympathetic direction.

The original text has quoted numerous passages from the Gītā, on the one hand, and from the Qur'ān, on the other. For the English rendering of passages from the Gītā, I have bodily incorporated into the volume the English version of them as given in the translation of the *Bhagavad Gītā* by Franklin Edgerton, Harvard Oriental Series. As for the English version of the passages from the Qur'ān, I have followed chiefly the translation of the Qur'ān by J. M. Rodwell, although here and there a few passages have been taken from the translations of M. Pickthal and Mawlavi Muhammad Ali. The passages embodied have, wherever found necessary, been revised in the light of the original text of the Qur'ān. In numbering the Qur'ānic verses quoted, I have adopted the order of arrangement observed in *Corani Textus Arabicus* edited by G. Fluegel, Lipsae, 1869.

SYED ASADULLAH

THE GĪTĀ AND THE QUR'ĀN

ALL RELIGIONS ARE AT THE BASE BUT ONE

Since the creation of the world, or at all events, since man began his life on this planet, the human heart has been pulled in opposite directions, sometimes toward selfishness, and sometimes toward the good of others. Evil and good, sin and virtue are but different names by which the two conflicting tendencies are known. No one is immune to this conflict. It is this internal tension which is the greatest of conflicts confronting man. Inability to eradicate selfishness or evil from within one's own mind amounts to an ignoble surrender to evil, and rising superior to evil or keeping it away from one's mind, a noble victory over it. The victory is noble because therein lies the good of all humanity, in as much as, it opens out the way to peace and progress on earth. The defeat is ignoble, because it involves man in acute personal distress, leading eventually to an all-round trouble for mankind. This is so, because mankind are bound one to the other, even as organically as the very organs of the human body; so much so, that it is not possible to differentiate the good of one from that of another. They all form together a family, and should therefore rest their inter-relationship on the bedrock of mutual love, sympathy and goodwill. Else, the least display of dislike and hatred between any of its members is bound to prove baneful to the family as a whole. So, to the extent man appreciates this truth or the fact of life that his own good lies in the good of all and that any harm done to another is harm done to one's own self, to that extent will he succeed in conquering the evil struggling in him for supremacy. Once this truth is realized and man begins to act upon it, the sense of exclusiveness in him gradually diminishes, and the sense of oneness expands, covering within its orbit, stage by stage, not merely his own hamlet or town or city and country, but the entire earth. He begins to feel that his own good lies in the good of others and reads in the distress of others his own distress. True peace and happiness, therefore, rests on a realization of this truth by one and all throughout the world.

But a realization of this character is by no means easy, particularly for individual nations. It is why mankind has stood divided against itself. The greater the zest for discrimination between one and anothar or for group formation, the greater the harm that is inflicted on the soul of human society. Dissensions breed sorrow and distress. In a word, the outer struggle which we notice all over the world is but a reflection or the result of the internal conflict raging within the mind of man.

The greatest effort made in the history of man to put an end to this struggle and instil in him the truth just referred to above has been done by dharma or religion. The term 'Dharma' is derived from the Sanskrit root 'Dhṛ' meaning 'to keep united'. Anything which keeps society together or prevents disintegration is dharma. This is the usual connotation attached to the word. In fact, the Mahābhārata states :

> "The term 'Dharma' is related to 'Dhṛ' meaning keeping together. It is due to dharma that people live together. So, whatever keeps people together is dharma. Dharma means the good of all. Whatever benefits all is dharma. Dharma is prescribed to protect from harm every living object. Every action which does not bring harm to any one is itsef dharma. He who always desires the good of all and is whole-heartedly engaged in doing good to one and all, O Jājilē! is one who knows what dharma is."

The word religion means 'the way'. The way of good to one and all is the real way or religion. The Qur'ān states:

> "Verily, this, your religion is the one religion, and I am your Lord; therefore serve Me;
> But they have rent asunder this their great concern among themselves into sects. All of them shall return to Us. (21: 92-93)

One day the Prophet was asked: "What is Faith?" He replied: "To exercise forbearance and to do good to others."

(Musnad Imām Aḥmed Ḥambal)

On another occasion observed the Prophet of Islam:

> "If one desires to be a Mōmin or man of faith, he should do good to his neighbour, and if he desires to be a Muslim, he should do unto others what he thinks is good for himself."
>
> (Tirmizī)

There is another saying of the Prophet which runs:

> "All mankind is the family of God, and he is the most beloved of God who does the greatest good to His family.
>
> (Bhaihaqi-Kitābal-'Imān)

'Panthī Mārg' or 'Path Mārg' in Sanskrit or 'tu' or 'du' in Japanese and Chinese languages, or 'madhhab' n Arabic, or religion in English, have the same connotation, viz. "that which keeps all united". The primary function of religion therefore is to protect humanity from internal dissensions and strife, to keep them together as a single family, and to show them the way to a united life — a life of good to one and all. This way of good living or the principle that it represents is nothing but what is universally recognised on all hands as the only way to good living, a way of life which the founders of all religions have consistently upheld through the ages.

To keep mankind on this straight path, all religions of the world have enjoined the belief in one Supreme God. There must be some being who controls this vast universe, and keeps it together and to which everything therein moves. Even as the rays of the sun and its heat reach this planet of ours and far beyond it, even so, there must be a store-house from where proceeds the life of everything and all the forces latent therein. Every religion has admitted that this being — call it Īśwara or Allāh - is beyond the comprehension of the limited intellect and understanding of man. At the same time, prophets, saints or rishis have claimed to break through their earthly frame and catch a glimpse of this Illimitable Being. Even religions of the type of Buddhism which do not admit of a Creator of the Universe, recognize that there is, in one form or another, the existence of a transcendental entity — Pūrṇa Àtmā, or Sarva Ātmā, "Perfect Soul", or Parama Ātmā, "Prime Soul", and suggest that it is the duty of man to strive for perfection and point out that the way to it lies through good living and fellow-feeling. In short, whatever name by which we call this Entity — Bhagawān, Īśwara, Parama Ātma, Khuda, Allāh or God, the essence of religion lies in believing in it as the Supreme Being giving life and sustenance to one and all, and on that basis living in brotherly ties with one another.

There is no doubt that the great religions of the world have kept millions of human beings, for thousands of years, on this straight path, and brought peace and happiness to their souls. In fact there has been no force stronger than religion which could bind the hearts of men.

At the present moment there prevail among mankind hundreds of creeds. Of these, six have the largest following — Hinduism, Judaism, Zorastrianism, Buddhism, Christianity and Islam. As far as investigation goes, Hinduism is regarded as the oldest, and Islam the latest. The followers of Hinduism are almost entirely confined to India. The largest number follow Christianity and the smallest Zorastrianism. Islam put in its appearance nearly 1350 years ago. Its followers number nearly 300 millions. Each of these six great religions has a Scripture of its own—the Ṛg Vēda of the Hindus, the Torah (old Testament) of Jews, the Zend Avesta of the Parsis, the Tripitaka of the Buddhists, the Evangel (New Testament) of the Christians, and the Qur'ān of the Muslims.

If we make a comparative study of the several scriptures, we shall notice that the basic truths presented by each are the same in every case. Some of the stories narrated therein and a good many of their expressions and passages appear to resemble one another creating on the mind of the reader the impression that these scriptures have proceeded from one common source. In fact, they will appear as but expansive branches proceeding from one and the same trunk, each in its own place and in its own time offering cooling shelter to many a weary wayfarer wandering in search of truth, and also solace and peace of mind to many a sorrowful heart.

Of the 6 scriptures referred to above, the Ṛg Vēda is regarded as the earliest, and the Qur'ān the latest. And yet in the chapter of the Qur'ān entitled "Light", the portion of it which form the praise of God and of His Almighty Power brings to mind parallel hymns of the Ṛg Vēda in praise of Īśwara.

The Qur'ān gives the Supreme Being the name of Allāh. In Ṛg Vēda, one of the names by which Īśawara is styled is " Ila' which has its root in 'Il' meaning 'to praise' or 'to worship'. A full 'Sūkta of Ṛg Vēda is an invocation to 'Ila'. Nearly 6000 years ago, in the language of Sumēria, 'El' was the term applied to God. The Sumērian city known as Babylon was really called 'Bab-El' or 'The Door of God'. The term is employed in several places in the Torah of the Jews and the Zend Avesta of the Parsis. When Christ was raised on the Cross, "Elai" "Elai" 'O My God' 'My God' were the words, he uttered. Mawlana Abul Kalam Azad has shown in his Tarjimān-Al-Qur'ān that it was this term by which, in one shape or other, God was referred to in the Hebrew, Syriac and Chaldean languages. The usual style was Iliha or Iloh. It is thus clear, that from the time of Ṛg Veda down to the present day, the term Allāh has in one style or another come to be applied to God.

Likewise, the 'Rab' of the Qur'ān is the 'Rai' of the Ṛg Vēda. The very first prayer in the Qur'ān: "Ihdinas Sirāt al Mustaqīm" or "Lead us on the Straight Path" exactly means the same as "Agnē Naya Supatha" in the Ṛg Vēda. The Vēdic "Ēkam Ēva Advitīyam" is the same as "Waḥdahu La S̲harika Lah" of the Qur'ān meaning: "He is One; there is none to associate with Him." A like resemblance is noticeable in other scriptures as well. 'Lā Ilāha Illallāh' of the Qur'ān 'There is no God but He' corresponds to "Nīst Yezdān magar Yezdān" of the Zend Avesta. One is the literal translation of the other. The phrase 'Bismillāh-ar-Raḥmān-ar Raḥīm' occurs 113 times in the Qur'ān. It means '(I begin) with the name of God who is merciful and compassionate.' The Zorastrian scholars begin their works with the expression "Ba nāmey Yezdān Bak-hṣhish Gardādār". Both bear the same meaning.

Let us now see what the great founders of religions have said of their forbears and of those who would come after them. If we carefully look into their utterances, we will find that all these great men have frankly and in plain terms endorsed the truth presented by every religion. Curiously their words in this respect have been neglected. Let us give a few illustrations:

> Srī Kṛiṣṇa says in Gītā: "In that way in which they worship Me, I give them Fruit accordingly. O Pārtha! whichever path is followed, a man ultimately comes and joins into My path." (4: 11)
>
> Says Zoraster: "We recognise the religions which were delivered in the past. They all directed men to goodness in life. (Yesna. 16: 3)

A vast majority of the Chinese people show an equal regard for the Indian Mahātma Buddha along with the Chinese 'Lao Tzo' and 'Kung Futze'. The last two were the founders of two great religions of China. Kung Futze said "I only ordain what has been in vogue in the past. I cannot invent anything new."

Said Buddha "Many Buddhas came before me and many will come after. I only spread the light of old."

The followers of Buddhism and Jainism believe that from the very beginning a series of "Buddhas and Tīrthaṁkaras (Guides) have come into the world to show but one and the same path of truth, and that similar guides will come after".

The Torah (Old Testament) says:

> "Is there any thing so novel about which it may be said: Lo Here is something new. All this has been there throughout the ages...... There is nothing new in the world" *

Said Jesus Christ:

> "Think not that I am come to destroy the law (the Law of Moses), or the prophets: I am not come to destory but to fulfil." (St. Mathew 4: 17)

* The original is not traceable for lack of proper reference. So, the Hindustani translation given in the work has been rendered here into English.

Such are the illustrations furnished by the world's scriptures. As a poet says:

> The difference is but of name!
> In reality, all are but one and the same, O friends!
> The transparent water that there is in the wave,
> It is only its refulgence that is reflected in the bubble.

II

In the above section, we have discussed the oneness of religions. In this section, we propose to deal with the well-known scriptures of Hinduism and Islam, viz., the Gītā and the Qur'ān. It is the followers of these two faiths who form the bulk of the population of India. When the Gītā was written, and what place it occupies among the sacred books of Hinduism, we shall point out in the section dealing with the Gītā. Likewise, in the section touching the Qur'ān, we shall state where, when and under what circumstances it was delivered and what influence it exerted on those among whom it was delivered. The Gītā is, as recognised on all hands, the quintessence of the Hindu faith. If the two sacred books are approached with an open mind, and without entertaining any predilections, it will be found that the basic truth which they impart is precisely one and the same.

The circumstances in which the Qur'ān was delivered in Arabia, and the Gīta in India were more or less parallel. In India the war of Mahābhārata was waged between the Pāṇḍavas and the Kauravas, members of the same family. In either rival camps, brothers, brothers-in-law and uncles of each other were intermixed. In like manner, the warfare, in the course of which, the Qur'ān was delivered, was a war between the members of one and the same tribe—the leading Arab tribe of the Quraish. Between the Quraish and Kauravas there is not only etymological resemblance but a historic similarity as well. 'Quraish' and 'Kauravas' are names which occur in the Iranian literature. One of the great kings of Iran bore the name of Kurus, which in English is distorted into Cyrus. The Iranians spell it as both 'Qurush' and 'Kuru'. In the Hebrew literature, this name appears as Quraish. The name of one of the leaders of Pāṇḍavas and Kauravas was Kuru. The term Kaurava is derived from 'Kuru'. It is a fact of history that the 'Kuru' and 'Kaurava' of the Mahābhārata and 'Kurush' or 'Kuru' of the Iranians, and 'Quraish' of Arabia are all derived from one and the same root.

Even as the Kauravas inflicted on the Pāndvas a variety of cruelties and gave them pain, seized their properties, turned them out of their homes, and pulled down their dwellings, burnt out their belongings, and tried to poison them, even so, the Quraish of Mecca perpetrated similar atrocities, and the Prophet Mohammad, his relatives and companions, who in response to his call, had discarded their ancestral idolatry and taken to the faith of Islam which insisted on the worship of none but the one God of all Creation. For thousands of years Mecca was the seat of an ancient temple. The Quraish were the priests or Pāndyas attached to it. The relatives of the Prophet persecuted him continuously for 13 years so much that he had to bid farewell to his own home-town, and betake himself to Medina. The Muslims who had already left Mecca to seek refuge somewhere, gradually congregated in Medina. A good number of Medinites welcomed the Prophet and joined the band of his followers. The Quraish of Mecca got infuriated. They resolved not to give rest to the Prophet. So, they intensified their persecution of the remnants of Muslims left behind in Mecca. At the same time a huge force invaded the Medinite territory with a view to exterpating the Muslims over there. Till this moment, it was not permissible in Islam to use arms even against the enemy. The verses delivered during the first 13 years of Islam repeatedly enjoined patience and forbearance towards the oppressors and to return good for evil.

> Moreover, good and evil are not to be treated as the same thing. Turn away evil by what is better, and lo! he between whom and thyself was enmity, shall be as though he were a warm friend.

> But none attain to this save men steadfast in patience, and none attain to it except the most highly favoured.
> And if an enticement from Satan entice thee, then take refuge in God, for He is the Hearing, the Knowing.
> (Q. 41 - 34-36)

> Turn aside evil with that which is better: we best know what they utter against thee.
> And say: "O my Lord! I betake me to Thee, against the promptings of the Satan:
> And I betake me to thee, O my Lord! that they gain no hurtful access to me. (Q. 23: 98-100)

When the Quraish invaded the territory of Medina permission for the first time was given by the Qur'ān to take up the sword in self-defence. The order ran in the following words:

> A sanction is given to those who, because they have suffered outrages, have taken up arms; and verily, God is well able to succour them: those who have been driven forth from their homes wrongfully, only because they say "Our Lord is the God." And if God had not repelled some men by others, cloisters, and churches, and oratories, and mosques, wherein the name of God is ever commemorated, would surely have been destroyed. And him who helpeth God will God surely help: for God is right Strong, Mighty: those who, if we establish them in this land, will observe prayer, and pay the alms of obligation, and enjoin what is right, and forbid what is evil. And the final issue of all things is unto God.
> (Q. 22: 40–42)

The Gītā styles the Kauravas as "ātatāyinah" or those who have fallen away from Dharma (Gītā 1: 36). In the Manusmṛti and other books "ātatāyinah" are described as those who are incendiary, poisoners. murderers, plunderers and those who commit excesses and prescribed death penalty for them. Manusmṛti enjoins: "kill the ātatāyinah at sight".

In the Qur'ān the term "Kāfir" is applied to those Quraish of Mecca who subjected the Muslims to diverse forms of persecution. The literary meaning, however, is "ungrateful". The Qur'ān advances three reasons for fighting these Kafirs of Mecca.

The first reason was that these Kafirs persecuted those who embraced Islam (Q. 4: 75). The second reason was that these Kafirs had turned out the faithful from their homes, simply because they had refused to worship images and would worship none but the one Supreme God of all mankind. And the third reason was that these Kafirs had now aimed to drive out the faithful even from Madina. (Q. 22: 40-42).

In this connection, what is noteworthy is that even as among the Kauravas and the Pāndavas, as already pointed out, there were in the rival camps of Arabs, members of the same family—brothers, uncles, both paternal and maternal, brothers-in-law and fathers-in-law intermingled on either side. Even as Arjun trembled at the thought of striking at his own people, and once actually refused to join the fray, even so, a good many Muslims were reluctant to strike their kith and kin on the other side. Even, as Srī Kṛṣna urged on Arjuna not to falter, saying:

> "Yield not to unmanliness, son of Pṛthā;
> It is not meet for Thee.
> Petty weakness of heart
> Rejecting, arise, scorcher of the foe!
>
> (G. 2: 3)

even so, noticing hesitation and disinclination to fight on the part of the followers of the Prophet, the Qur'ānic words were delivered:

> "War is prescribed to you: but from this ye are averse. Yet haply ye are averse from a thing, though it be good for you, and haply ye love a thing though it be bad for you: And God knoweth; but ye, ye know not.
>
> (Q. 2: 212-213)

Just as Kṛṣna tells Arjuna:

> Either slain thou shalt gain heaven,
> Or conquering thou shalt enjoy the earth
> Therefore arise, son of Kunti,
> Unto battle, making a firm resolve.
>
> (G. 2: 37)

even so, does the Qur'ān tell the followers of the Prophet:

> "Let those then fight on the path of God, who barter this present life for that which is to come; for whoever fighteth on God's path, whether he be slain or conquer, we will in the end give him a great reward." (Q. 4: 77)

Fighting for Dharma or Nyāya is called Dharma Yuddha or war for Dharma. In the Qur'ān, fighting for the protection of religion and justice is called 'Qittāl Fī Sabīlillāh' or fighting in the way of God. It so happened that in both the cases, victory was for those who fought for Dharma, and in both cases war was the only way to help the cause of Truth.

So far, we have shown how similar, one to the other, is the teaching of the Gīta and the Qur'ān. We shall now deal with the identity of principles which both have propounded. We shall give below a few illustrations from the Qur'ān and the Gīta, as also from other works held in high regard respectively in Hinduism and in Islam, and also quote from the sayings and writings of saints and seers, bhaktas and sūfis, to establish the basic oneness between the two religions.

We shall first present the concept of Īśwara or Allāh. The Gītā and the Qur'ān hold exactly the same view of Him. Īśwara is styled by Gītā as the Light of Lights (G. 13: 17) and the Light of the sun and the moon (G. 7: 8) The Qur'ān calls Allāh the Light upon Light (Q. 30: 5) and the Light of the heavens and the earth (Q. 30: 5).

According to the Gītā Īśwara carries people from darkness toward light (G. 10: I1). Likewise, the Qur'ān speaks of Allāh as He who carries people from darkness toward light (2: 257). In the Upaniṣads the oft-recurring prayer is "Lead us from darkness into light". The Prophet's wellknown prayer is: "O! God give me light."

In the Gītā, Īśwara is called one whose countenance (Viśvatō Mukham) is noticeable in every direction; and the Qur'ān says: Wheresoever ye turn, ye shall find the countenance of God (Q. 2: 115). The Gītā calls Īśwara the Lord of the Worlds (G. 5: 29). The Qur'ān too calls Allāh Lord of the Worlds. (Q. 1: 1)

The Gītā calls Īśwara Satya (17: 23) and the Qur'ān calls Allāh Al Ḥaq (22: 62), both meaning "The Truth". The Gītā speaks of Īśwara as "None like unto Him" (11: 43); the Qur'ān says exactly the same: "None like unto Him" (Q. 112: 4). In the Śwētāśvatara Upaniṣad of Yajurvēda, God is described as " one who has no equal or with none superior to him "

The Gītā says: "The entire world is encompassed by Īśwara (9: 4, 11 : 33). The same is stated in the Īsa Upaniṣad: Whatever thre is in this world is encompassed by Īśwara ". The Qur'ān says: " verily Allāh encompasseth all things." (Q. 41: 54).

The Gītā says of Īśwara as the beginning of all living objects, their middle and their end (10: 20). The Īśa Upaniṣad of Yajurveda says: " He walks and He does not walk; He is far and He is near; He is inside of every thing and outside of everythnig ". The Qur'ān speaks of Allāh: " He is the first; He the last; He the manifest and He the Hidden; and He is the knower of all things (Q. 57: 3).

The Gītā speaks of Iśwara as 'Akṣara' or 'never to be obliterated, and of all else as Ksara or that which is to be obliterated (I5: 16). The Qur'ān says " All on the earth shall pass away; but the countenance of thy Lord shall abide resplendent with majesty and glory. (Q. 55: 26-27).

Gītā speaks of Īśwara as " Acintya " or 'beyond wisdom' (G. 2: 23) Anirvacanīya or 'one whom words fail to describe in words' (G. 3: 43). The Qur'ān speaks of Allāh as " Vision comprehends Him not; and He comprehends all visions " (Q. 6: 104). Many more are the attributes of God, which the Gītā dwells upon in more or less the same language as employed by the Qur'ān.

If we look into what the Hindu and Muslim seers have had to say of the attributes of God, the resemblance between the Gītā and the Qur'ān becomes clearer. Says the Gītā:

Of a thousand suns in the sky
If suddenly should burst forth
The light, it would be like
Unto the Light of that exalted one. (G. 11: 12)
Devouring them Thou lickest up voraciously on all sides
All the worlds with Thy flaming jaws;
Filling with radiance the whole universe,
Thy terrible splendors burn, O Viṣṇu! (Q. 11: 30)

The famous poet Shams Tabrez of Iran addresses Allāh in the following words:

" Oh! light of my eyes, my mind and my soul! Thou art the Kind who occupieth the throne of my heart. Thy light is like

> the combined light of millions of Suns and Moons shining from beyond space. Thou alone art stationary; and Thou alone art in motion; Thou art the Essence and Thou the thousand forms it assumes; Thou art below and Thou art above; Thou alone art the body; Thou alone the spirit. The Truth has kindled a Fire, It is burning out untruth. That fire burns out the heart. May it burn out my heart!

Muṇḍak Upaniṣad says: "It is His light which has lighted the world. It is through His refulgence that the world is refulging."

Even as the Gītā and the Qur'ān regard God as beyond the comprehension of man, so does a sufi poet say:

> "He is beyond the limits of our thought and imagination;
> We can only exercise our mind within its limits."

In the Kēna Upaniṣad of Sāma Vēda, it is said: "He who says that Īśwara is knowable, does not know him. He who knows that he cannot know Īśwara, knows Him. Those who claim to know Him, know Him not. They alone know Him, who do not claim to know Him."

The idea that God encompasseth all things has been expressed by a Muslim sufi thus:

> Whatever we see in the K'aba or the Cathedral, is what love's fancy has wrought.

In the Gītā, the thought often recurs that Īśwara lives in the heart af His worshippers (18 - 61). In certain places occurs the expression; "Īśwara dwells in the hearts of His devotees" (10 - 11) and also: "They who ardently worship Me, they live in Me, and I in them". (9: 29).

The Prophet has said "The heart of man is the seat of Raḥmān, the God of compassion."

The Śatapatha Brāhmaṇa of Yajur Vēda says: "Īśwara lives in the heart of man; It is why the heart is called Hṛdaya".

Mawlana Rumi in his Mathnawī, generally called the 'Qur'ān in Persian' writes:

> "The Prophet says: "Says Allāh; I cannot be contained beneath the earth or above it, neither in the heavens nor on the 'Arsh', but I dwell in the heart of the Momin (Viśwāsī Bhakta) or believing devotee. He who cares to seek me out, let him seek me out there."

Śiva Stōtra states: "I dwell neither in Kailāsa nor in Vaikuṇṭha, my habitation is the hearts of sincere devotees."

A Muslim sūfi expresses this idea in the following beautiful lines:

> " He is in my heart and my heart is in his Hand,
> Even as the mirror is in my hand and I am in the Mirror.

Another sūfi says:

> " O thou forgetful! wither wouldst thou wander? Look into thy heart.
> The fairy is there in the mirror which thou holdest in thy bosom. "

In the Gītā, the manifestations of God are described variously. Says Srī Kṛṣṇa:

> I am taste in water, son of Kunti,
> I am light in the moon and sun,
> The sacred syllable (Ōm) in all the Vēdas
> Sound in ether, manliness in men.
> Both the goodly odor in earth,
> And brilliance in fire am I,
> Life in all beings,
> And austerity in ascetics am I. (G. 7: 8-9)

What is called 'Vibhūti' in the Gītā is called 'Mazhar' or manifestation of God in Sūfi literature. The Sūfi work, Gulshan-i-Rāz, states: " All Phenomenal objects in the universe are each a manifestation of Allāh." What in Gītā is called "Viśva-Rūpam" or "Virāt Rūpam" is called in Islamic literature "Shakle Moḥīt" (circumference). Believing God in this way is called by the Sūfi, Muraqaba-i-Iḥata-i-Kulli or total comprehension. Mawlana Rūmī says in his Mathnawī:

> " I am the sweetness in the sugar, the oil in the almond — Sometimes I become the crown of Kings — sometimes the consciousness of the Conscious, and sometimes the indigence of the indigent."

Says the Gītā:

> The (sacrificial) presentation is Brahman; Brahman is the oblation;
> In the (sacrificial) fire of Brahman it is poured by Brahman;
> Just to Brahman must he go,
> Being concentrated upon the (sacrificial) action that is Brahman. (G. 4: 24)

A Muslim sūfi expresses the same idea in the following lines :

He himself is the cup and himself the cupmaker,
Himself the clay of it, and Himself the one who drinks out of it.
He it is who buys the cup; and
He it is who breaks it too and gets away."

In respect of the relation that subsists between God and the phenominal world, says the Gītā :

Who see Me in all
And sees all in Me,
For him I am not lost,
And he is not lost for Me.
Me as abiding in all beings whoso
Reveres, adopting (the belief in) one-ness
The abiding in any possible condition,
That disciplined man abides in Me. (G. 6: 30-31)

The well-known Muslim sūfi writer of the 12th century of the Christian era, Muḥiyuddīn Ibn 'Arabi writes: "Do not look at God as anything apart from His creation, and do not look at creation as anything apart from God."

It is this concept of God which gives rise to the twin theories of 'Dvaita' and 'Advaita' in India or the 'Vahadat al Shuhūd' and 'Vaḥadat al Vajūd. Certain scholars connect Vaḥadat al Shuhūd not with Dvaita but with Viśiṣṭādvaita. According to Ādvaita or Vaḥadat al Vajūd point of view, whatever is noticeable or that there is in the Universe is itself God and that there is nothing therein but God, and that whatever else we may notice or see is Māyā or illusion. It is this idea which is at work in expressions such as 'Ahaṁ Brahma' or 'I am God' 'Sarvaṁ Khalvidaṁ Brahma' or 'All this is Brahma' or 'Anal Ḥaq', 'I am the Truth' and 'Hama Ūst', 'All is He'. As against this view, 'Dvaita' or 'Vaḥadat al Shuhūd' means that Īśwara or Allāh has a being of His own and that matter or creation has a separate being. They are all created by God, but are not God. The Muslim terms this 'Hama Az Ūst', the phenominal world is from Him. The supporters of either view are to be found both among the Hindu and Muslim scholars.

The curious thing to note in this connection is that the advocates of both the views freely quote from the same source, the Gītā on the one hand, and the Qu'rān, on the other, in their support.

We do not propose to enter into any philosophic discussion of the subject. It is enough for us to point out that the Gītā and the Qur'ān are freely invoked by the protagonists of both the divergent theories.

In the Gītā, it is stated that He who worships Īśwara in sincere devotion, transcends all limitation and becomes Brahman (G. 14: 26). In the language of the sūfis, this is called Fanā Fillāh or 'losing one's identity in God'. [1]

The concept of God apart, there are a number of issues on which the Gītā and the Qur'ān express identcal views. We shall only touch upon a few of them.

In respect of the rise of the universe or of its birth, Gītā states that all living objects in the beginning were in a state of Avyakta or unmanifestation, when none of them was yet formed or had taken a shape or put on any colour. It is only in the transitional stage (Vyakta) that they manifested their characteristics. Ultimately, they will return to the original state of Avyakta or cease to exist. But this is not a matter to worry about (2–18). The Qur'ān says:

> "We all are Allāh's and to Him shall we return."
>
> (Ch. 2: 156)

The sūfis have expressed this in a clearer language. In the language of Islam, Avyakta is called 'Adm' or non-existence. A sūfi poet says:

> "We were in a state of non-existence and we shall return to the same state."

For nothing, do we witness the intervening play. Mawlānā Rūmi referring to the Qur'ānic words referred to above (2: 156) says:

---

1 In his work 'The Gītā and the Qur'ān', Muftī Saiyyid Abd'l Qayyūm Jallandari commenting on the statement of Srī Kriṣṇa that he is himself Īśwara, states " Kishenji divesting himself from his human nature or individuality is here speaking from the station of Fanā Fillāh or absorption in Godhead or the state of Brahman. Even like him certain muslim saints have in a state of 'intoxication' burst out into similar utterances which are apparently against the law of shar'a ".

> All forms have emerged from that which is formless (Nirākār) Avyakta and return to the same formless Being (Nirākār).

Chāndōgya Upaniṣad says : The phenomenal world emerges out of the same Avyakta viz. Īśwara. Subsisting on Him it puts on diverse forms and eventually merges back into the very same Avyakta.

In respect of the Soul, says the Gītā : "Neither the sword can cut it, nor fire burn, neither water can soak it nor dry it up" (8 : 23). Mawlānā Rūmi says in his Mathnawī.

> The qualities of the body change;
> But the soul abides like the bright Sun;
> Why worry over the thought of death when the soul is deathless."

Touching the subject of Rebirth Srī Kṛṣna says in the Gītā.

> You and I have had many a rebirth. I am aware of them, while you are not. " (G. 4 : 5)

There is nothing definitely or clearly stated in the Qur'ān to contravene the idea of Rebirth. On the other hand, there are verses in the Qur'ān which seem to lend support to it. It is on the basis of such verses that two conflcting views are held among Muslims on the subject — (1) in favour of Rebirth (2) the other against it. Here are a few verses which may be cited in favour of the idea of Rebirth :

> He it is who gives ye life;
> Then He causes you to die,
> Then He will bring you to life.
> And it is he who will give ye life once again,
> Verily man is ungrateful. (Q. 2: 66)
>
> Verily God causeth the grain and the date stone to put forth : He bringeth forth the living from the dead, and the dead from the living ! This is God ! Why, then, are ye turned aside from Him ? (Q. 6 : 96)
>
> How can ye withhold faith from God ? Ye were dead and He gave you life; next He will cause you to die; next He will restore you to life ; next shall ye return to Him ! (Q. 2 :26)
>
> It is we who have decreed that death should eb among you; We are not thereby hindered from replacing you with others, your likes, or from producing you again in a form which ye know not !

> Ye have known the first creation: will ye not then reflect?
> (Q. 56: 60)

It is on the basis of these verses that thirteen out of twenty four sects of Shi'ā Muslims believe in the doctrine of Rebirth. In addition to these a good many Muslim scholars and sufis (as for instance, Mawlānā Rūmi, Ibn al Ṭufail, Ibn Khaldūn and Imam Ghazālī) have supported the doctrine. We shall quote only from Mawlānā Rūmī:

> Like grass, I have grown many a time and have changed my form seven hundred and seventy times.

Māwlānā Rūmi was a believer in the theory of evolution. Some of his well-known lines may be reproduced here:

> I died as a mineral and became a plant,
> I died as plant and rose to animal,
> I died as animal and I was man.
> Why should I fear? When was I less by dying?
> Yet once more I shall die as man; to soar,
> With angels blest; but even from angelhood
> I must pass on: all except God doth perish
> When I have sacrificed my angel-soul,
> I shall become what no mind e'er conceived.

Take another item of resemblance between the Gītā and the Qur'ān. Prophets or Avatāras were born in all climes, countries, and ages, and delivered their common message of righteous living in all languages. This fact has been endorsed both by the Gītā and the Qur'ān. Śrī Kṛṣṇa says in the Gītā:

> For protection of the good,
> And for destruction of evil-doers,
> To make a firm footing for the right,
> I come into being in age after age. (G. 4: 8)

The Qur'ān says:

> And when their apostle came, a rightful decision took place between them, and they were not wronged. (Q. 10: 48)
>
> And in order that He might speak plainly to them, we have not sent any Apostle, save with the speech of his own people; but God misleadeth whom He will, and whom will He guideth: and He is the Mighty, the Wise. (Q. 14: 4)
>
> Apostles truly have we already sent before thee and wives and offspring have we given them. Yet no apostle had come with

miracles unless by the leave of God. To each age its Book. (Q. 13: 38)

Verily we have sent thee with the truth; a bearer of good tidings and a warner; nor hath there been a people unvisited by its warner. (Q. 35: 24)

We send not our Sent Ones but as heralds of good news and warners; and whoso shall believe and amend, on them shall come no fear, neither shall they be sorrowful. (Q. 6: 24)

Let us now consider the differences which exist between religions. Says the Gītā:

In whatsoever way any come to Me,
 In that same way I grant them favour,
My path follow
 Men altogether, son of Pṛthā,

The Qur'ān says:

To every one of you have we given a rule and a beaten track. And if God had pleased He had surely made you all one people; but He would test you by what He hath given to each. Be emulous, then, in good deeds. To God shall ye all return. (Q. 5: 48–49)

All have a quarter of the Heavens to which they turn themselves; but wherever ye be, hasten emulously after good: God will one day bring you all together; verily, God is All powerful. (Q. 2: 143)

Says a sūfi poet:

"Every one is after the same beloved, the sober and the drunk alike.
Every place is the abode of love, be that a mosque or a temple."

Puṣpadantāchārya says in Mahimna Stōtra:

"In accordance with their different dispositions, people take to straight or curved paths in search of Iśwara. But they all tend towards Him, even as all rivers, by taking different routes, reach one and the same ocean."

A sūfi says:

"Kufr and Islam both hasten along thy path, affirming that there is but one God and has no associate."

So far, we have dwelt on the close identity between the Gītā and the Qur'ān. It is quite possible that here and there we may come across things which are not common to the two. We shall in the pages to follow point out what is common to all religions or at least to what is clearly identical in the Gītā and the Qur'ān or where they do not differ from each other. One may indulge in philosophic or theological disquisitions in respect of each of the two. But in regard to the basic duty of man, what it is, and how to fulfil it, what obstacles lie in the way of its fulfilment, and how to get over them, and how by overcoming them, we shall prosper in the world and obtain salvation in the world to come — in respect of these, all scriptures, particularly the Gītā and the Qur'ān, hold but one and the same view. We shall illustrate this by quoting from both the scriptures.

Some of the passages from the Gītā which bear on this subject are reproduced below:

Doing My work, intent on Me
Devoted to Me, free from attachment,
Free from enmity to all beings,
Who is so, goes to Me, son of Pāṇḍu, (G. 11: 55)

Brahma-nirvāṇa is won
By the seers whose sins are destroyed,
Whose doubts are cleft, whose souls are controlled,
Who delight in the welfare of all beings. (G. 5: 25)

So the wise man should act (but) unattached,
Seeking to effect the control of the world. (G. 3: 25)

By comparison with himself, in all (beings)
Whoso sees the same, Arjuna,
Whether it be pleasure or pain,
He is deemed the supreme disciplined man. (G. 6: 32)

After creating creatures along with (rites of) worship,
Prajāpati (the Creator) said of old;
By this ye shall procreate yourselves —
Let this be your Cow-of-Wishes. (G. 3: 10)

Good men who eat the remnants of (food offered in) worship
Are freed from all sins;
But those wicked men eat evil
Who cook for their own selfish sakes. (G. 3: 13)

The greatest Dharma is to engage oneself in the service of others. This is emphasised by the sacred books of Hinduism. The Purāṇas state:

> "The wearing of Tulasi beads, the putting on of a mark on the forehead, the smearing of ashes over the body, the going on pilgrimages, the taking of dips in holy waters, the performing of 'havan', the doing of penance or the offering of Darśana to priests in temples will not wash one's sins. It is the good done to others that cleanses the soul."

In another place say the Purāṇas:

> In all the 18 purāṇas taken together, Vyāsa has said but two things, and they are:
> Doing good to others is virtue: and to cause harm to others is sin."

A Hindi poet says:

> In the four vēdas and six Śāstras only two things are mentioned:
> "To cause pain is to feel pain;
> To cause happiness is to feel happiness."

Tulsidas says:

> "O brother! there is no religion higher than
> doing good to others;
> And no sin greater than causing pain to others."

The Qur'ān repeatedly advances the views:

> "God truly loves those who do good to others."
> "Say: Come, I will rehearse what your Lord hath made binding on you — that ye assign not aught to Him as partner; and that ye be good to your parents; and that ye slay not your children because of poverty; for them and for you will we provide: and that ye come not near to pollutions, outward or inward: and that ye slay not anyone whom God hath forbidden you, unless for a just cause. This hath he enjoined on you, to the intent that ye may understand.
>
> And come not nigh to the substance of the orphan, but to improve it, until he come of age: and use a full measure, and a just balance: We will not task a soul beyond its ability. And when ye give judgment, observe justice, even though it be the affair of a kinsman, and fulfil the covenant of God. This hath God enjoined you for your monition —"

And 'this is my right way'. Follow it then; and follow not other paths lest ye be scattered from His path. This hath he enjoined you; that ye may fear Him. (Q. 6: 152-154)

O Believers! stand up as witnesses for God by righteousness: and let not ill-will at any, induce you not to act uprightly. Act uprightly. Next will this be to the fear of God. And fear ye God; verily, God is appraised of what ye do.

(Q. 5: 11)

What! thinketh he that no one regardeth him?
What! have we not made him eyes,
And tongue, and lips,
And guided him to the two highways?
Yet he attempted not the steep.
And who shall teach thee what the steep is?
It is to ransom the captive,
Or to feed in the day of famine,
The orphan who is near of kin, or the poor that lieth in the dust;
Besides this, to be of those who believe, and enjoin steadfastness on each other, and enjoin compassion on each other.
These shall be the people of the right hand:
While they who disbelieve our signs,
Shall be the people of the left.
Around them the fire shall close. (Q. 90: 7-20)

Woe to those who STINT the measure
Who, when they take by measure from others, exact the full;
But when they mete to them or weight to them, minish—

(Q. 83: 1–3)

Worship God, and join not aught with Him in worship. Be good to parents, and to kindred, and to orphans, and to the poor, and to a neighbour, whether kinsman or new-comer, and to a fellow traveller, and to the wayfarer, and to the slaves whom your right hands hold; verily, God loveth not the proud, the vain boaster. (Q. 4: 40)

What thinkest thou of him who treateth our RELIGION as a lie?
He it is who thrusteth away the orphan,
And stirreth not others up to feed the poor.
Woe to those who pray,
But in their prayer are careless;
Who make a shew of devotion,
But refuse help to the needy. (Q. 107: 1–7)

> If ye make reprisals, then make them to the same extent that ye were injured: but if ye can endure patiently, best will it be for the patiently enduring.
>
> Endure then with patience. But thy patient endurance must be sought in none but God. And be not grieved about the infidels, and be not troubled at their devices; for God is with those who fear him and do good deeds.
>
> (Q. 16: 127–128)
>
> They prefer them before themselves, though poverty be their own. (Q. 59: 9)

The Qur'ān points out that they have lived successful lives who have tried first to meet the wants of others before they could satisfy their own wants.

There are numerous verses in the Qur'ān where injunction is given to do good to one's enemies. Indeed, even in respect of one's treatment of those to fight whom in self-defence permission is given, the following caution is offered:

> But when all is over, then take to the chase: and let not ill-will at those who would have kept you from the sacred mosque lead you to transgress, but rather be helpful to one another according to goodness and piety, but be not helpful for evil and malice: and fear ye God. (Q. 5: 3)

Says a sūfi poet:

> The way of God-realisation is nothing but the way of service to mankind.
>
> Neither is it beads, nor prayer-carpet nor the garb of the pious.

The poet Sayeed says:

> To lessen the pain of some one is more important than offering a thousand prayers at each station on your pilgrimage to Mecca.

Another sūfi says:

> To win one's heart by rendering service to hin is the greatest Haj. A heart so won is better than a thousand Kalabas.

Innumerable quotations of this character may easily be cited from the writings of the sages of every country and religion.

The question is how to discharge this duty. The Gītā and the Qur'ān emphasise that 'every one of our deeds is to be offered for God alone'. Īśwarārpaṇa (May it be for God) is the term employed to convey the sense.

On Me all actions
Casting, with mind on the over-soul,
Being free from longing and from selfishness,
Fight, casting off thy fever. (G. 3: 30)

Casting (all) actions upon Brahman,
Whoso acts abandoning attachment,
Evil does not cleave to him,
As water (does not cleave) to a lotus-leaf. (G. 5: 10)

Whatever thou doest, whatever thou eatest,
Whatever thou offerest in oblation or givest,
Whatever austerity thou performest, son of Kunti,
That do as an offering to Me. (G. 9: 27)

Likewise, the Qur'ān employs the term "Fī - Sabīl Allāh–in the way of God or for the sake of God."

> They who expend their wealth for the cause of God, and never follow what they have laid out with reproaches or harm, shall have their reward with their Lord; no fear shall come upon them, neither shall they be put to grief. (Q. 2: 266)
> And as for him who of his own accord doeth what is good — God is Grateful, Knowing. (Q. 2: 153)

The Gītā says:

Whatever thou doest, whatever thou eatest,
Whatever thou offerest in oblation or givest,
Whatever austerity thou performest, son of Kunti,
That do as an offering to Me.

The Qur'ān says:

> My prayers and my worship and my life and my death are unto God, Lord of the Worlds. He hath no associate. This am I commanded, and I am the first of the Muslims. (Q. 6: 163)

In the well-known Arabic work "Al Qawl Al-Jamīl", it is stated: "The traveller on the road to God must always keep God in mind while reading or talking, eating or drinking or walking".

The Gītā and the Qur'ān both enjoin that man must discharge his duty by rising superior to happiness and sorrow, success and defeat, and to the result of his actions. Such an attitude is called by Gītā "Niṣkāmakarma" and by the Qur'ān 'Iqlas'.

Says the Gītā:

On action alone be thy interest,
    Never on its fruits;
Let not the fruits of action be thy motive,
    Nor be thy attachment to inaction.
Abiding in discipline perform actions,
    Abandoning attachment, Dhanaṁjaya!
Being indifferent to success or failure;
    Discipline is defined as indifference. (G. 2: 47–48)

The Qur'ān says:

And commemorate the name of thy Lord, and devote thyself to Him with entire devotion. (Q. 73: 8)

In his Tafsīr or Commentary of the Qur'ān, Imam Razi while explaining the sense of the verse just quoted above says:

He who looks for a reward for his good deeds, or desires to be saved from the results of bad actions is not a person who remembers God disinterestedly. His prayar or contemplation of God is not for God alone. But he who offers his worship to God and does everything for God alone, he indeed is a true devotee of God.

The Gītā says:

Not interested in the fruit of action,
Who does action that is required (by religion)
He is the possessor of both renunciation and discipline (of action);
Not he who builds no sacred fires and does no (ritual) acts. (G. 6: 1)

A Muslim saint, Sūfiān Sūrī says:

"It is not piety to put on rough clothes or eat dry bread Piety lies in conquering one's desires."

The Gītā says:

Casting (all) actions upon Brahman,
    Whoso acts abandoning attachment,
Evil does not cleave to him,
    As water (does not cleave) to a lotus-leaf. (G. 5: 10)

The Qur'ān says:

"He Who depends entirely on God, God is sufficient for him."

The Gītā says:

> " He who rivets his mind on results, entangles himself in the meshes of Karma."

Shāh Waliullāh of Delhi observes:

> To love any objects beside God is to drop a screen between God and himself. If we do not turn away from them, we have achieved nothing."

The pursuit of anything in the way of God is fraught with difficulty. It is not easy to say what forms it assumes. Mawlānā Rūmi furnishes an answer:

> " All trouble proceeds from lust and vain desires.
> Else; this world is a place full of sweet nectar."

In reply to Arjuna's questions: " What exactly is that which compels a man to commit a sin against his own inclination, Sri Krishna says:

> It is desire, it is wrath,
> Arising from the strand of passion,
> All-consuming, very sinful;
> Know that this is the enemy here. (G. 3: 37)

What is the method by which lust and anger can be kept in check? The Gītā and the Qur'ān suggest one and the same mëthod: It is to keep one's mind under proper restraint.

The Gītā says:

> Them all restraining,
> Let him sit disciplined, intent on Me;
> For whose senses are under control,
> His mentality is stabilized. (G. 2: 61)

The Qur'ān states:

> God desireth thus to turn him unto you: but they who follow their own lusts, desire that with great swerving should ye swerve! God desireth to make your burden light: for man hath been created weak. (Q. 4: 32)
>
> And who goeth more widely astray than he who followeth his own caprice without guidance from God? for God guideth not the wicked. (Q. 28: 50)

In like manner, the Qur'ān says:

> And who master their anger, and forgive
> Others! God loveth the doers of good. (Q. 3: 128)

The Gītā says:

> This is of hell the threefold
> Gate, and ruins the soul:
> Desire, wrath, and greed:
> Hence one should abandon these three. (G. 16: 21)

The Qur'ān uses for 'evil desire' the term "Ḥawā" and repeatedly warns us to beware of it. "Bādiā according to the Qur'ān is a part of hell where dwell those whose good deeds weigh lighter than their evil deeds.

> And as to him whose balances are light — his dwelling-place shall be the pit. (Q. 101: 9)

Says, Bu Alī Shāh Qalandar:

> He alone is man who conquers lust, averice, and evil desires;
> Anger and lust blind the man!

They side-track him from the straight path. In Islam 'Anger' is 'Harām' or prohibited, and therefore, it is prohibited to do a thing, good or bad, under the stress of anger. A noble illustration is furnished from the life of Hazrat Ali, son-in-law of the Prophet. In a battle he got better of his opponent. He quartered him and sat over his chest and with his sword drawn, he was at the point of striking him when the fallen foe spat at his face. Instantly Haḍrat Ali threw away his sword, and said to him "Now, I shall not strike thee", and straightaway stepped aside. The man felt bewildered and asked: "Why did you spare my life?" Replied Haḍrat Ali: "I was fighting for the sake of God and not for my sake. When you spat at me, I was roused to anger, and anger is 'Harām', 'Prohibited'. To do anything under its stress is sin."

Many a spiritual practice have been devised to control one's passions. They are more or less the same as suggested by the Qur'ān and the Gītā. But we need not go into their details. To keep under control one's thought also is an equally important step in the process. Says the Gītā:

> Who has no desire towards any thing,
> And getting this or that good or evil
> Neither delights in it nor loathes it,
> His mentality is stabilized.

And when he withdraws,
As a tortoise his limbs from all sides,
His senses from the objects of sense,
His mentality is stabilized. (G. 2 : 57–58)

What the Gītā calls "sthitaprajña" the Qur'ān calls "Qalbi-Muṭmainnā" or Nafs-i-Muṭmainnā", the heart which is at peace with itself. The Qur'ān is full of praise of such a heart.

"Those who believe, and whose hearts rest securely on the thought of God. What! Shall not men's hearts repose in the thought of God? They who believe and do the things that be right—blessedness awaiteth them and a goodly home."

(Q. 13 : 28)

"When he brought to his Lord a perfect heart, When he said to his father and to his people, What is this ye worship?"

(Q. 37 : 82)

The Prophet Muhammad says: "Real good is for him whose heart is reserved for faith in God, whose heart is at peace with itself, whose tongue speaketh truth, whose disposition is equable, whose ears listen, and whose eyes see."

(Shu'ab Al'Imān—page 51)

Referring to the term 'Salīm' or Equable, a Muslim scholar writes: "When man is immune to the promptings alike of joy and sorrow, and of worldly desires, he becomes 'Salīm' or one living at peace with one's own self or one equable in disposition." The Gītā states:

"When his mind is not perturbed in sorrows,
and he has lost desire of joys,
His longing, fear, and wrath departed,
He is called a stable-minded holy man." (G. 2: 56)

It is stated in Manu Smṛti "He alone is Jitēndriya (One who conquers his self) who is neither pleased nor displeased with what he hears or touches or beholds or eats or drinks or smells". The Gītā states:

"He will not rejoice on attaining the pleasant,
Nor repine on attaining the unpleasant;
With stabilized mentality, unbewildered,
Knowing Brahman, he is fixed in Brahman."

(G. 5: 20)

It is statd in the Qur'ān :

> "Lest ye distress yourselves if good things escape you, and be overjoyous for what falleth to your share. God loveth not the presumtuous, the boaster." (Q. 57: 23)

In the city of Basra, there lived a famous Arab lady, Rabi'a, who was a sūfi. Once Jafar Bin Sulaimān put the qucstion to her: "When is God pleased with his servant?" She replied, "When man is calm in moments, alike of joy and pain". An Iranian poet says:

> "Neither did joy ever elate me, nor sorrow depress,
> Joy and sorrow come to me as but visitors and pass away."

To the extent man achieves control over his passions, and gains peace of mind, to that extent does he realize himself, strengthen his spirituality, and get nearer to God.

Says the Gītā:

> "To those who have put off desire and wrath,
> Religious men whose minds are controlled,
> Close at hand Brahma-nirvāṇa
> Comes, to knowers of the self" (G. 5: 26)

Likewise, there is a saying of the Prophet Muhammad "He who has realized his own self has indeed realized God."

It is stated in Śatapatha Brāhmaṇa that Yājñavalkya while engaged in instructing Janaka said: "Probe thy soul: you will find therin a solution to everything. The one way to find a solution to the riddle of life is to understand one's own soul." Says Mawlānā Rūmi: "He who beholds and recognises himself, he will take rapid strides towards perfection."

The same idea was advanced in the Bṛhadāraṇyaka Upaniṣad by Yōgi Rāj Yājñavalkya.

Said Hadrat Alī: "O man! your ailment is in you, but you do not notice it, and its remedy also lies in thee and you are not aware of it."

The Gitā says:

> "One should lift up the self by the self,
> And should not let the self down;
> For the self is the self's only friend,
> And the self is the self's only ememy."

"The self is a friend to that self
By which self the very self is subdued;
But to him that does not possess the self; in enmity
Will abide his very self, like an enemy." (G. 6: 5-6)

The Qur'ān says:

"Blessed now is he who hath kept it pure.
And undone is he who hath corrupted. it" (Q. 91: 9-10)

A well-known tradition of the Prophet runs: "Your greatest enemy is your own self."

Dhun-nūn of Egypt was a great sūfi. He had heard that a woman sūfi was a great devotee of God. Dhun-Nun went to her and asked for guidance. She said: "Keep thy passions under restraint, and keep thy heart clean like a mirror." "Sister! say something more." She said: "Question thyself in respect of thyself."

In the world's scriptures, no greater stress is laid on anything than that laid on the need for keeping one's heart and mind under control. In fact, the process of control has been raised to the status of a science. It is called "Yōga" among Hindus, and "Sulūk" among Muslims. The Sadhus and the sūfis have extracted pure nectar in the process. A careful study of works dealing on the subject will convince the reader that the method pursued in the Hindu and Muslim way is but one and the same or, to put it in different words, is made of the same texture. We shall offer a few illustrations in support of this contention and close this section of our discourse.

In both the methods, stress is laid on the need of a Guru or Pir or Preceptor. Such is the reference to it both in the Qur'ān and the Gītā.

The Gītā says:

"The (sacrificial) presentation is Brahman;
Brahman is the oblation;
In the (sacrificial) fire of Brahman it is poured by Brahman;
Just to Brahman must he go,
Being concentrated upon the (sacrificial) action that is Brahman." (G. 4: 24)

The Qur'ān says: "But follow the way of him who turneth unto me." (Q. 31: 14).

Mawlānā Rūmi says: "He who wants the companionship of God must first seek the company of the friends of God or men of God (Awliā).

In sūfi books a 'Guru' is called 'Murshid' or 'Rahbar'. In all such books emphasis is laid on the need of seeking a Pīr. He is defined in them as one who possesses a balanced mind, "Sthitaprajña". The Prophet Muhammad said: "The sign of a Rahbar is that, if one comes across him, instantly the thought of God should come to him". In India, Kabir and other saints and Mahatmas have frequently pointed to the need of a true Guru for every seeker of God.

It is said in the Qur'ān that the Prophet Moses once felt the need for a guide or a Guru. The guide tested him thrice, and on every occasion Moses failed to fulfil the test; and yet it was from him alone that Moses had to learn the truth.

> "Then found they one of our servants to whom we had vouchsafed our mercy, and whom we had instructed with our knowledge.
>
> And Moses said to him, "Shall I follow thee that thou teach me, for guidance, of that which thou too hast been taught?"
> He said "Verily, thou canst not have patience with me;
> How canst thou be patient in matters whose meaning thou comprehendest not?".
>
> He said, "Thou shalt find me patient, if God please, nor will I disobey thy bidding."
>
> He said, "Then, if thou follow me, ask me not of aught until I have given thee an account thereof." So they both went on, till they embarked in a ship and he - the unknown - staved it in. "What!" said Moses, "hast thou staved it in that thou mayest drown its crew? A strange thing now hast thou done." He said, "Did I not tell thee that thou couldst not have patience with me?"
>
> He said, "Chide me not that I forgot, nor lay on me a hard command."
>
> Then went they on till they met a youth, and he slew him. Said Moses, "Hast thou slain him who is free from guilt of blood? Now hast thou wrought a grievous thing!"
>
> He said, "Did I not tell thee that thou couldst not have patience with me?"

> Moses said, " If after this I ask thee aught, then let me be thy comrade no longer; but now hast thou my excuse. "
>
> They went on till they came to the people of a city. Of this people they asked food, but they refused them for guests. And they found in it a wall that was about to fall and he set it upright. Said Moses, " If thou hadst wished, for this thou mightest have obtained pay. "
>
> He said, " This is the parting point between me and thee. But I will first tell thee the meaning of that which thou couldst not await with patience. "
>
> " As to the vessel, it belonged to poor men who toiled upon the sea, and I was minded to damage it, for in their rear was a king who seized every ship by force.
>
> As to the youth his parents were believers, and we feared lest he should trouble them by error and infidelity.
>
> And we desired that their Lord might give them in his place a child, better than he in virtue, and nearer to filial piety.
>
> And as to the wall, it belonged to two orphan youths in the city, and beneath it was their treasure : and their father was a righteous man : and thy Lord desired that they should reach the age of strength, and take forth their treasure through the mercy of thy Lord. And not of mine own will have I done this. This is the interpretation of that which thou couldst not bear with patience. " (Q. 18 : 64-82)

Numerous instances of this nature are recorded in Hindu scriptures where it was risky to pursue the path of Yōga without a Guru.

In the Gītā references are made in various places to the subject of Yōga and methods of pursuit are described.

The Gītā says :

> " Let the disciplined man ever discipline
> Himself, abiding in a secret place,
> Solitary, restraining his thought and soul,
> Free from aspirations and without possessions ."
>
> (G. 6: 10)

In the stanzas following the one just quoted above, the Gītā describes how a Yōgi should sit erect in a clean place, concentrate his gaze on the tip of his nose and think of Īśwara. Yōga literally means " to meet ". So Yōga is the means of meeting God.

In Islam, Yōga is called 'Sulūk' and Yōgi 'Sālik'. The Prophet Muhammad once praised a hermit who in a cave was engaged in contemplation of God (Abu Said Khuzrī).

Among the sūfis are observed various forms of Sulūk and contemplation (Samādhi). The practice is called 'Shaghal' (Abhyas). Those who observe such practices trace them to some verse or other of the Qur'ān. There are over 50 different practices described in sūfi works and nearly all of them are more or less of the same variety as observed in Hindu Yōga. One of these sūfi practices is styled 'Sūltan Mubīn or Sultan Mahmūd' in which concentration is revetted on the tip of the nose even as described in the Gītā. Among these practices, there is one which requires concentration on the spot midway between the two eye-brows called in Hindu scriptures 'Brahmanidhar'. Another practice is to concentrate on the centre of the heart. In respect of these practices, an Arab sūfi poet states: "Sit on your heart even as a sparrow sits on its eggs so that you might feel wonderful experiences."

A form of yōga called 'Prāṇāyāma' is referred to in the Gītā (8: 12; 4-29 and 30). The Muslim sūfis call Prāṇāyāma as Ḥabs-e-Dam (breath control). These two terms convey one and the same meaning. It is also called Habs-e-Nafs. Shah Waliullah in his book Al-Qawl-ul-Jamīl, describes in detail those methods of Ḥabs-eDam which tally with the spirit of the Qur'ān. As the Hindus sometimes concentrate on 'Om shabd Parchat' while performing Prāṇāyāma, so do the Muslim sūfis concentrate on 'Allāh' in the region of the heart while practising Ḥabs-e-Dam. In this book in which several methods of devotion are described, the one which is called Shaghl-e-Bisāth is also dealt with. Under this method, the eyes are closed, the tip of the tongue is raised to touch the ceiling of the throat, in the same manner as in the Kaichari Mudra of Haṭa Yōga and an attempt is made to enclose the breath at the base of the brain.

The results of these practices are described in Al-Qawl-ul-Jamīl. In another book of the sūfis, viz., Ḍia-ul-Qulūb (The Light of Hearts), many methods of Ḥabs-e-Dam are described. By one of these methods, breath is controlled and the eye-sight.

is fixed between the two brows. In another method, the gaze is turned toward the sky.

By one particular method of yōga, called 'chat', the mind is withdrawn from 'the without' or external objects and concentrated on 'the within'. It is stated in the Gītā that salvation is attained through devotion to Īśwara and by exercising control over the senses.

In his Mathnawi, Mawlāna Rūmi writes: "Close your eyes, your lips and your ears, and if you fail to discover the secrets of God, laugh at me."

The study of both the Hindu and Muslim books on the subject of Yōga or 'sulūk' will show that they are replete with methods of devotion – Abhyāsa or Ashghal. There is probably no Abhyāsa or Shaghal which in one form or other is present in one and is not to be found in another.

III

We have shown above that there is so much of unity between one religion and another, particularly, between the Gītā and the Qur'ān in basic matters. But this unity is not reflected in the relations observed between the followers of the two faiths. On the other hand, we notice that religion is being employed not for welding humanity into a single family, but for cutting it into rival groups, each living in conflict with every other. It is a matter for great sorrow that, so far, no solution has been found to remedy the evil.

And why so? The questions which arrest attention are: What are those natural urges which help man live a good life, and what are those which cause him harm, and consequently need to be kept in check? What is society? What are its basic needs, and wherein lies the good of the individual and of society as a whole? For these and similar questions the founders of religions, — avatāras and prophets — have no doubt supplied solutions, but the solutions offered by them are conceived from a plane not easy to be reached by the common man. These solutions in themselves are true and valuable; but the path of life chalked out by them is by no means easy for the ordinary man to pursue. Still, the fact stands that there is no solution other than what they have offered for the happiness of man. At all events, so far as spiritual progress is concerned, there is really no other guidance except the one provided by religion.

And what is this solution? The solution may be said to consist of a few plain straightforward truths. The basic among these is the idea of one Īśwara or one God. The Gītā and the Qur'ān present a living picture of this Being. If there is but one Creator for the entire Universe and there is no other beside Him to exercise control over it, how is it that in the objects created by him, there should subsist so much of coflict and discord? Does not all this suggest that those who profess to believe in this one God of the Universe in reality do not entertain that belief. A few earnest souls there have always been in human society - Sadhus, Saints, Sūfis and Faqīrs - who have never been happy over this state of affairs. Such people have lived in all ages and in all countries. They cannot believe that those who really believe in God could live in perennial conflict with each other, or in the field of action run counter to to the commandments of God. It is why Avatāras, Prophets, Tīrthaṅkaras and men of high spirituality have arisen from time to time to bring man back to the path of true religion and to God. Their efforts, it is true, have not altogether eradicated the evil that we have referred to, but they have undoubtedly shown the way to spiritual progress and good living.

The aim of these great souls has been two fold. On the one hand, they have raised before the human mind a vision of the true God and stimulated the sense of devotion to Him. On the other hand, they have tried to cleanse social life by rooting out false forms of worship, injustice and selfishness, so that mutual hatred between man and man might be removed and the spirit of fellow feeling restored, and the world helped to live like a single family.

THE GĪTĀ AND THE QUR'ĀN

In the history of our country, we can point to a glorious galoxy of great souls who have worked for the good of society—Kabīr, Dāwūd, Tukārām, Nānak, Chaitanya, Muīnuddīn Chistī, Bāba Farīd, Meera, Nizamuddin Awlīa, Reydas, Bhulle Shāh and others. They threw light on the deepest aspects of the Oneness of God or Divine Unity. They fought evil and injustice wrought in the name of religion, and condemned them in no uncertain terms. A perusal of their writings not only acquaints the reader with the high principles which guided their lives, but stimulates in him the urge to respect truth, to serve his fellow men, and develop true spirituality. We propose to give a few passages from the writings of one or two of this great band of spiritual men just to show what great part they have played in bringing happiness to society. These passages will give the reader an idea of the chains with which evil customs have bound man and how they should be cut asunder.

KABĪR

In the following lines, Kabīr not only refers to the unity in ideas that subsists between the Gītā and the Qur'ān, but draws a beautiful picture of the unity that should subsist between the Hindus and the Musalmans of the land. It hurts his tender soul to find man keeping aloof from man and raising walls of differences between them — differences in eating, and drinking, differences in stations of life, differences in matters of marriage, and differences in methods of worship. He bevails over these differences in a voice that pierces the heart of his hearers. Addressing the Muslims and Hindus of his time he says:

> "O Brother! how can there be two masters or two gods for this single world?
>
> Say, who has given thee this wrong idea?
>
> Allāh and Rām, Karīm and Kēśav, Hari and Haḍrat are but different names given to one and the same Being, even as different jewels are made out of the same gold. The two are not separate things. One calls it Namāz, the other Puja. Mahadev

> is the same as Muhammad. Brahma is Adam. Who is Hindu and who is Musalman? Both live on the same Earth. One reads the Vēdas, and the other, the Qur'ān. One is called Mawlāna, the other is called Pandit. The vessels are different, though they all are moulded out of the same clay.

Kabīr says:

> Both are simpletons, both are misled. None of them has found God. One slaughters the goat, the other, the cow. In the pursuit of such vain differences, they have wasted their lives".

Referring to the differences over the Mosque and the Temple and over the question whether to turn, to the East or West at the time of prayer, Kabīr says:

> " If God lives in the Mosque, who then lives in the rest of the world? All the Hindus think that Rām lives in the Tīrth and in his images; but they have not found Rām. Those who think that Īśwara is in the East and Allāh in the West are in profound error. If they want to find Him, they must seek Him in their hearts. They will find Him there. The same is Karīm, the same is Rām. The Vēdas and the Qur'ān are not false books. They are false who in the name of the two books neglect to think and reflect. The man who finds the same Allāh in every human being and who looks upon every other as he looks upon himself cannot do harm to anyone. The women and men who live in the world are all of your appearance. Says Kabīr: The man who refers to Rām and Allāh as but one and the same, he is my Guru, he is my Pīr (Guide)."

Kabir looks upon the entire mankind as but one people. Says he:

> " The entire world is labouring under a great harmful delusion. One swears on the Veda, and the other on the Qur'ān. One speaks of hell, another of heaven. There is really no difference between the two paths. The soul of a man and the soul of a woman are of the same texture. Their bodies are moulded out of the same earth. There is but one and the same life in both. When their bodies are obliterated, the differences in their outward features also will disappear. The unthinking have gone astray. Human beings are of one species. They all possess the same type of skin, the same type of bones, the same type of excreta, the same kind of

blood, and the same kind of flesh. They all have come out of a single drop. No one is Brahman; and no one is Shudra. Brahma, Viṣnu and Mahēṣa are the names of three states of the same soul - animation, calmness and sloth. Says Kabīr: All must love the one God of all. There is no one who is a Hindu, no one who is a Musalman. The difference between the two is a false difference ".

Referring to the outward form of customs and rituals, says Kabīr:

" O People! when a man dies, what do you do with his body? The moment he breathes his last, you take his body out of your house. One burns it, another buries it. The Hindus do the former; the Muslims the latter. The result is the same. Both discard the body and go their way." "The Hindus avow that the name of their beloved is Rām, the Musalmans give to their beloved the name of Rahmān. The two fight with each other over a name and finish themselves. The Reality neither knows."

Kabīr looks down upon all distinctions of caste and of touchability and untouchability.

" The in and out of every one is of the same cast. None is Brāhmaṇa none Sūdra. All talk of high and low castes is vain, and no one should indulge in it. The idea also is vain that the Hindus and the Musalmans are two different peoples. They are all but one.

DĀWŪD

The writings of Dāwūd are full of similar observations. A few examples may be given here: Says Dāwūd.

" The same is Allāh; the same is Rām; the same is self-sufficient; the same is Master of all. The different names by which He is called are but like different dishes prepared out of the same flour. One chooses what is agreeable to him. O Dāwūd! that Beloved has countless names. Call Him by any name you choose. Good people make no distinction between these names. The Hindus say: Our way is the right one. The Musalmans say: our way is the right one. Ask these people to show which way is the way of God. The two people have both strayed away from the real path. People favour duality, favour separate ways. But this duality is false. God likes only truth. O simple folk! Think over! Whither are you going, and how long will you thus go? These people have cut Īśwara into pieces and distributed them between themselves. O Dāwud! All these people have strayed away from "Pūrṇa Brahma", the one Allāh, and fallen a prey to delusion. O Dāwud! Only one and the same spirit dwells in all. In every one the same Īśwara dwells. It is only by virtue of this relation to Īśwara, We shall have to relate ourselves to one another. We should not entangle ourselves in the differences of outward forms and groups. O Dāwud! Both the Hindus and Musalmans are in error. Both are foolish. With proper care one must follow the real track whereon no one should be a stranger to another. These people have drawn water from the same well and stored them in different vessels. The illusion of duality they must throw off."

Dāwūd says further:

"The illusion that Allāh and Rām are separate entities is now off my mind. I see no difference between a Hindu and a Musalman. O Īśwara! I see Thy glory in every one. The breath in each is one and the same breath. The body of every one is moulded in but one form, each has in his veins the same kind of blood and in his body the same kind of flesh and the same kind of eyes. One and the same life is at work in every one. The ears of every one receive the same sounds. The sweet tastes sweet to every tongue. One and all feel the same type of hunger. In each case, it is satisfied in one and the same manner. All have the same type of bones and joints. Joy and sorrow affect them in but the same way. Pain is pain to them all. All have the same style of hands and feet, the same style of bodies. The whole drama is staged by one and the same Creator. He alone is the creator. He alone has enabled me to see him in every thing. It is by beholding Him that way alone, that Dāwūd has brought tranquility to his soul."

Speaking of the essence of religion, says Dāwūd:

"To efface the self, to worship the One Īśwara, to protect one's body from evil activity and one's mind from evil thought, to wish no ill-will of any living object — these, O Dāwūd! constitute the essence of religion. That person is alone holy, 'Sant', who entertains no ill-will towards any living object. O Dāwūd! there is only one spirit in all beings.

No one is our enemy. We have found this out by careful search. No one is alien to us. Whether we are Hindus or whether we are Musalmans, one and the same spirit dwells in all. By giving separate names to men and women, we have cheated ourselves. Hindus and Musalmans are brothers to once another. They form the two hands, the two feet, the two ears, and the two eyes of the same body. In the mirror of suspicion only, we look as but two beings. It is an illusion. Once this illusion is dispelled and suspicion rooted out, the talk of otherness will end. O Dāwūd! Against whom do you entertain ill-will? Is there any one here beside yourself? The God who brought me into being, the same dwells in every one."

Referring to the differences over the mosque and the temple, says Dāwūd:

"The Hindus are attached to the temple, the Musalmans to the mosque. I am attached to Him who has no fixed abode. I think I am every moment living with God. I neither need a temple nor a mosque. There He is present of His own accord. The devotion to Him calls for no particular ritual. The true Guru, may guide, has shown me that this very body of mine is my mosque and my temple. Within it alone, man can offer all his devotion to God. For that, he need not go out of it. The Hindus and the Muslims look like two mad elephants. They do not therefore drink together from the same pool. By discarding their separateness, they can together live a united life. O Dāwūd! Unconcerned with the 'thine' and 'mine' of the two, wilt thou remember that Holy Master of all who is above this squable of 'thee' and 'me'. I am for him who, by effacing his self, sings alone of Iśwara. O Dāwūd! the two people are obsessed by their sectarianism, and are therefore torn assunder. Do not keep their company. They are going the wrong road, the road of ruin.

Speaking of the presence of God in every one, Dāwūd says:

"Even as oil is pressent in the oil seed, the pleasant smell in flowers, and butter in milk, even so, God is present in every soul. He is present in every soul, as the soul is present in every nerve of each body. Even as light is present in the Sun and coolness in the Moon, even so, the God who has made of our heart a temple, He alone dwells therein. In every heart, the beloved alone is seated and no one else".

Speaking of the different names by which Allāh is known, says Dāwūd :

> My son ! None lives at once in two places.
> The One hath many names.
> There is none but He.
> The Absolute is but one, call Him Rām or Rahim.
> Thou alone art Mohana, Thou, Keśava, Karīm.
> Thou art the Creator; Thou art the pure.
> Thou the Establisher, Thou the Omnipresent.
> Thou alone the Nourisher ; Thou alone the Holy
> Thou alone the Almighty ; Thou alone the king
> Thou the ever lasting Allāh, the self-subsisting
> Thou art without similitude
> O Dāwūd, all mean but the One

GURU NĀNAK

In this connection, the devotional hymns of Guru Nānak and Guru Gōvind Singh deserve mention. The founder of Sikhism, Guru Nānak, came into prominence in the last days of Kabīr. Even like Kabīr and Dāwūd, he had both Hindus and Muslims among his disciples. Guru Nānak was himself a great lover of Kabīr, so much so, that in the religious book of the Sikhs, the Adhi granth, the names of Kabīr and other Muslim saints and Faqirs are mentioned along with Guru Nānak. Sikkhism took its rise as a synthesis between Hinduism and Islam. When Guru Arjun wanted a holy man to lay the foundation stone of the Gurudwāra at Amritsar, he approached the famous Muslim saint, Mian Mīr, for the task. It is he who formally laid the foundation stone of this famous Gurudwāra.

Guru Nānak, saddened over the Hindu Muslim tensions of his time, says :

> I am neither a Hindu nor a Muslim. The devil of otherness is goading both of them on to mutual rivalry. Say : neither the Hindu nor the Muslaman is finding his way. The two fight each other by regarding Rām and Rahīm as but two different entities. The two do not really believe in the one God of all ".

Says Guru Gōvind :

> " One calls himself 'Mandia', another Sanyāsi, or Yōgi or Brahmacāri or Jaṭi. One calls himself Hindu, another Musalman : one calls himself Shia, another Sunni. These differences are false. There is only one caste for all human beings. They all are equal. There is only one God for them all. He alone is their Creator. He alone the Karīm, the doer of good; He alone the Razzāk, the provider of nourishment; He alone the Rahīm, the one who shows mercy to one and all. No one has any God beside Him. All this difference is illusory. Him alone must all worship. He alone is the holy guide of mankind. All mankind are moulded in but one shape. In every one, the same spirit of God is at work. He who is in the Mandir is also in the Mosque. What is Pūja is what is Namāz.
>
> All mankind is but one entity. It is merely an illusion to distinguish one human being from another. The terms Dēvata, Adēv, yakṣa, Gandharva, Hindu and Musalman and so forth are born of customs and manners prevalent in the different parts of the world. All have the same style of eyes, ears, bodies and tongues. Everybody is composed of the same elements, earth, air, fire and water. He who is Allāh is himself Abhēd. What is in the Purāṇas, the same is in the Qur'ān. All have the same appearance and the same shape."

So far, we have presented the views and observations of a few of the sages of India on the emphasis which religion laid on the Unity of God and on the broad requisites of human society. These sages, it may be pointed out, have also expressed themselves, at times very strongly, on the weaknesses prevailing among the followers of the different religions. We set forth here a few illustrations :

Referring to the question of untouchability among the Hindus, Kabīr observes :

> " O paṇdit ! You accept water from another's hand only after you have ascertained to what caste he belongs. Remember, that the house of clay wherein you now sit is the same clay into which all creation on earth has to lie one day. In this very clay, 56 crores of Yādavas and 80,000 Munis have lost their identity and become one with it. Under every foot

of ground lies buried a prophet, one and all reduced to dust.
O Paṇḍit! You are a vessel moulded out of this very clay. Still you do not accept water from another's hand, till you have ascertained to what caste the other belongs. In the water that you draw from a river, countless snails and frogs live. Their blood and the matter that comes out of them are mixed up with this water. The dirt of the world flows into this river. Dead bodies of human beings and animals float thereon and rot. Where does the milk that you drink come from? What you call milk is what percolates from flesh and bones of an animal, You perform 'Sudhi' for your mud pot, and fancy that you have purified it.

O Paṇḍit! give up your habit of quoting from Vēdas and Sāstras in support of your weaknesses. They are all inventions of your mind. O Paṇḍit! you have read your Vēda and forgotten it. You have not found yourself. You perform Saṅdhyā, Tarpaṇa, Gāyatri and a variety of Karma Kāṇḍa. In the process, you have spent your life. Still, you have not attained salvation; for you sprinkle water over yourself whenever you touch a human being and you fancy you have purified yourself. Tell me who is of the lowest order except you when you avoid the touch of a human being. You fancy you belong to a high order and you feel proud of the thought. But no good will come to you. Iśwara who is Garva Prahārī, the Crusher of Pride, how can He tolerate your pride? Salvation is for him only who discards from his mind every thought of birth and caste, even as a seed annihilates itself in the earth to spring up into a lovely plant.

Addressing a Brāhmaṇa who avoids the common touch, says Kabīr:

"O Paṇḍit! I feel sad that when someone in your house or some neighbour dies, you feel you have contacted impurity. You then cook 'Rasuit' of a dead goat and then you take your bath, perform puja and put on your Yajñōpavīta across your shoulder and then you sit for your meals. There are bones in your cooking pot. There are bones of dead animal in the plate before you. Say what sort of Dharma Karma is this? Whenever you talk of Dharma, at that very moment you take the life of another. O Brother! This is not good. If I should call you Brāhmaṇa, whom may I have to call butcher?

"O Santu! Listen! This world is suffering under a delusion. Very few understand that one Paramātma dwells in every body". Says Kabīr:

The Hindus and the Musalmans in the name of their religion are intent on enjoying the pleasures of the tongue. Referring to this, says Kabīr:

> "O Santu! I have looked into both the ways. The Hindus and the Musalmans are intent on following their own way. Both are caught in the snares of the pleasures of the tongue. The Hindus observe Ēkādaşi; they gather their relations around them and make feast of milk and sweets. They discard food, but they indulge, without measure, in all tasty things. The Musalmans observe fast. At dusk they perform Namāz and then proceed to eat away an entire plate of fowl. This is not the way to go to heaven. The Hindus have rooted out love for others from their hearts. The Musalmans have given up loving others. One eats what is called 'Halal', the other what is called 'Jhataka'. The luxury of the tongue is indulged in either case. The true Guru has told me that the Hindus and the Musalmans must have but one way." Kabīr says: "O Santu! Listen! There is no difference between Rām and Khuda. But both the Hindus and the Musalmans have gone astray."

Describing false religious leaders, says Kabīr:

> "O Santu! The world is getting mad. Speak the truth, and people rush at you to strike. Everyone puts implicit faith in what is false. I have seen many a religious person. They get up early in the morning; they take their bath and kill a living object and eat it, and worship an image carved out of a stone. These people have no sense. Similarly, I have seen many a 'pīr' who read the Qur'ān. What way will they show to their disciples when they themselves do not know the way. Gurus of this type abound here who, applying ashes to their body, seat themseleves in a deceptive pose. In their hearts they feel they are great persons. But they bow before images made of brass and stone. They are fond of pilgrimages. They wear beads round their neck and put on the hermit's cap over their necks, apply pompous 'tilak' to their foreheads and sing hymns. But they are not aware of what is within them. The Hindus say Rām is their God, the Muslim ssay Rahīm is their God. The two fight each other and perish. No one knows Reality. In their false sense of holiness, they go round from house to house and preach 'Mantrams' and collect disciples. The Guru and the disciple alike will go under and come to grief." Says Kabīr: "O Santu! All this

is deception. How often am I to remonstrate? Few people care to listen to truth. Iśwara lives equally well in everyone. The real Qāzi is he who sets things right, and will not agree to wicked deeds. He who induces others to evil action is not a Qāzi. On the other hand, he is a 'pāji' (evil doer). O Kabir! The real Guru is one who feels the pain of others in himself. He who does not feel the pain of others is not a 'Pīr or Guru. He is Kāfar or be-Pīr (or guideless)."

Referring to quarrels over temples and mosques, says Dāwūd:

"The Mandir which the Hindus raise with their own hands is looked after by them with great care. But the body of a man or an animal which is the Mandir raised by Iśwara himself they destroy. Similarly, the Musalmans show respect to the Mosque raised by their own hands, but they pull down the structure raised by God himself. The true Guru has pointed out to me that the body of man alone is the Mosque or Mandir of God. Living within that body, we have to worship Allāh. There is no need for us to go out of it to worship Him. Within the human heart lies, full to the brim, the fountain of Iśwara's Being. We can freely purify ourselves in its water and perform our ablutions with it and offer Namāz. This body is our Mosque or Mandir. Our five senses form the congregation therein; our mind is the leader in prayer, or Imām. In our own body we may bow before Allāh and hail Him."

Referring to image-worship, says Dāwūd:

"They carve out an image out of stone and give it the name of Iśwara. O Dāwūd! True Iśwara is not discernable to them. It is why the world is going wrong. Rām dwells in the soul of every one. One must worship Him. True Bhaktas love the Rām within them. O Dāwūd! The true devotee is one who worships the beautiful God in him."

Referring to the outward show of worship and attendant ritual, says Dāwūd:

"O Dāwūd! the ritual of the Vēd Sāstras is to keep people in chains. That is why the true worship of the Master cannot be offered from the heart. Many have become Musalmans and many have become Hindus in this world.

"O Dāwūd! Devotion to Iśwara is only true devotion. The rest is vanity and false pride. One must regard his body a holy scripture. In that book is written the name of Īśwara. One must regard his soul as his Paṇḍit, and from that Paṇḍit let him learn the name of Īśwara written in that Book. Let him write down the name of Rahmān in that Book and with his mind as his Mulla (i.e. Paṇḍit) let him pray to Rahmān."

Referring to religious customs, Dāwūd says:

"People do not know the true Rām. They all see things which are not true — false gods, false devotion, false worship, false offerings, false devotees, false food, false ecstasy, false pardah, false clapping, false listeners, and false stories. People believe in these false things, and call upon others to put faith in them. The Light of Īśwara shines in every object, both animate aud inanimate (Jal-thal Mahel) O Dāwūd! In every soul only Rām dwells. He is Ever Living."

Explaining what true religion is, says Dāwūd:

"The true devotee is he who sings the songs of the one Īśwara, who keeps his mind under control, who does not show pride, who does not lie, nor does harm to any one, but abstains from doing a wicked deed and does good to others, who never looks upon any one as his enemy, who looks on others even as he looks on himself, but contributes to others' happiness and looks upon all with an equal eye, who does not let his interests interfere his relations with others, who does not differentiate between with his interests and the interests of others, and seeks in one and all the light of the One Holy Providence, who always speaks truth and is immersed in his own thoughts, who unmindful of every danger engages himself in devotion to God and to no one else. Dāwūd! such people are but few in this world."

IV

For thousands of years, voices have been heard to the effect that all those who live on earth form a family. We do not know of any religion which has not placed this vision before its followers. There has been no Mahātma or Sūfi or Faqīr whose one ardent wish has not been to see raised to the ground the walls erected to divide man from man. The trend of nature is also in the same direction. It is carrying humanity forward toward such consummation. It is stated in the Vēdas: "Let there be one purpose before us all; Let you all develop one mind; your good lies in that. You act together, eat and drink together. Īśwara desires you to fulfil together the great purpose. The soul force of the world is pulling us on toward that destination. You move together even as the wheels of a charriot. Speak with one voice. Let the minds of all work in union and grasp the one Truth. The coming dispensation whose vision the vedas have raised before us has been looked forward by every religion; and each has in its own way worked for it. Keeping in view the entire galaxy of Prophets who have come into the world to contribute to this vision in all ages and in all countries, addresses the Qur'ān:

> And surely this your community is one community, and I am your Lord, so keep your duty to Me.
> But they became divided into sects each party rejoicing in that which was with them. (Q. 23: 52-53)

Says the Bible:

> Be of one mind, live in peace; and the God of love and peace shall be with you (Corinthions 13: 11). God does not distinguish between man and man, whatever his nation God loves him who fears Him, and does good. (Acts of Apostles)
> There is neither Jew nor Greak, there is neither bondman nor free, there is neither male nor female; for ye are all one in Christ Jesus (Galations 3: 28).

The Mahātma of China, Kung Futze has said:

> "Learn to live in amity with your neighbours, and love your brothers (Shuking)."

Mahātma Buddha has said:

> "What are these moving figures of human beings? They are the hands and feet of the same body. So, each part must look after every other part."

The well-known Hindu religious saying runs:

> "This is mine and that is another's! Only small men entertain the distinction. But those who have large hearts, regard every one living on earth as a member of one's own family."

The books on religion are replete with this type of teaching. Still, the world of man is far off from the goal envisaged. The reason for it is twofold. One is that a good many people do not understand the truth offered. The other is that even those who appreciate the truth do not care to follow it. The responsibility for the setback in the march forward does not rest on those who do not understand the truth. The entire responsibility lies on those who knowingly do not follow it. It is by action that revolutions or great changes have been wrought. The study of the Gītā and the Qur'ān is not simply meant to provide food for the intellect. On the other hand, it is meant to spur us on to right action. Our aim is to see that the two holy books should be read with this purpose in view. The purpose of our study should be to invoke God to inspire in us the force which shall shatter all the chains of selfishness born of our attachment to one's family, village, country, nation and sectarian creed which have kept us divided and which incite us to fight each other. It is not enough to feel or think that we all are one. On the other hand, what we need is the zest to eradicate from our life, both individual and collective, the evil which has worked for division among us, whatever their nature—social, legal or religious.

We do not need any new religion now. The religion of heart, of humanity — the religion on which all religions rest should suffice for us. We now need a new society, a new culture in which the spirit of humanity and not the spirit of this or that group, shall prevail — a society in which man should live and move on terms of equality with brother man, and whose laws shall not subserve the evil of discard. We need an order of life which shall raise itself on the solid foundations of mutual love and co-operation. We need a religious outlook which shall wield us into a single brotherhood, nation, family. This new religious outlook, this new nationhood, shall not, like the prevailing religions, as practised among us, promote hatred between one another. Our creed should be a creed of humanity, love and sacrifice. That is the creed which every Avatāra, Prophet, Saint, Sadhu, Faqir has preached — the true Dharma or Mānu Dharma, Al-Din.

We pray to God that He will inspire in the followers of the Gītā and the Qur'ān that clear thinking, that courage and that strength which shall enable them to act upon the pure teachings which the two holy books offer for the guidance of man and help them to fashion afresh a new type of culture and a true religious outlook, so that a wave of love might spread across the entire country of ours. There is no other way of salvation for us!

THE GĪTĀ

Those books which the Hindus regard as their scriptures may not be in thousands; but they can easily be counted by hundreds. Among the existing religions of the world, probably no one claims to possess so many scriptures as does the religion of the Hindus. It is but natural that they all resemble one another and appear to have taken their rise from one common source and constitute the links of but a single old chain. They are just like separate flowers grown on branches spread out in all directions and sprung from the single trunk of a huge tree. So far as the history of the different families of faith are concerned, the Hindu line is probably the oldest in the world. The Semitic family of faiths is of a late origin. The Chinese faith, as far as the available knowledge of its rise goes, is not older than that of the Hindus. Besides, the Hindu faith did not face the upheavals which the faith of China experienced during the course of the last two and a half thousand years. At any rate, it escaped catastrophes.

Several thousand years before the rise of the Indian and Chinese civilizations, several great nations had emerged and reached the highest pinnacle of progress. The written and unwritten records clearly indicate that from the Persian mountains down to the Arabian sea and the Indian ocean on one side, and along the banks of the Nile in Africa on the other, at least two great nations existed for long in ancient times and led the world for several thousand years in the art of living. But now, only traces of their ruins are occasionally brought to view by patient exploration and research. Having transmitted what vitality they could to cultures which succeeded them, they disappeared altogether from the scene of life. But the fact stands that among the scriptures available to-day, the Ṛg Vēda is the oldest. We need not enter into a discussion as to which of the ten thousand and five hundered and eighty verses of the Ṛg Vēda are the earliest. A comparative study of all the existing religions will reveal that they have originated from Īśwara or Allāh and that the source of all scriptures, as mentioned in the Qur'ān, is with Allāh Himself. The major part of rites and rituals together with the names and words of worship are found in the Ṛg Vēda, more particularly in its early verses. European scholars are thus led to believe that the Ṛg Vēda is the mother of all religions.

Among the books of the Hindu faith, the Ṛg Veda is held int he highest esteem. But Vēdas are so bulky, their language so archaic and unfamiliar, and the methods of reciting each mantram so varied that even to scholars, the Vēdas have been for thousands of years, a huge problem; and they are likely to continue to be always so.

The Upaniṣads are considered to be the gist of the Vēdas, and are in fact selections from the latter. The Upaniṣads, more particularly the twelve Upaniśads which together do not constitute even a small book, contain high principles of moral idealism. They deal with good and evil and the intricate problems of transcendental metaphysics, and the deeply spiritual guostic issues touching God and Soul. The Upaniṡads therefore occupy a high place among the holy books of the world. If the educated Hindus are asked what scriptures they would like to preserve from destruction in times of chaos and revolution for the future guidance of mankind, they would certainly point to the Upaniṣads. Indeed, thousands of non-Hindus will endorse such a decision.

But the Upaniṣads are not intelligible to the common reader. Scholars only can understand them.

Next to the Upaniṣads, the most popular book with the Hindus is the Srīmad Bhagavadtgītā.

The language of the Gītā and its treatment are so simple, that the book commands a much larger number of readers than the Upaniṣads. The simile of the cow and its milk is repeatedly applied to the Upaniṣads and the Gītā. The simile appears to be very appropriate. In the commentaries on the Gītā, it is said that one who has memorised or mastered the Gītā need not go to any other scriptures of the Hindu faith. The Gītā is, in fact, the essence of all the existing scriptures of the faith, and its popularity among the Sanskrit books is incomparable. Barring the Qur'ān, there is scarcely any other scripture on which so many commentaries have been written during the past several thousand years, as on the Gītā. There is no doubt that at least among the existing books in India, the Gītā constitutes the finest flower of the Hindu culture. Among the few books that enjoy respect beyond the confines of countries to which they belong, and furnish their guidance and grace to other countries and nations at all times. The Gītā of India occupies an honoured place. It is one of the imperishable works of the world.

The problems of human life have been the same in all countries and in all ages, despite their varied forms and the names given to them from age to age. There has always been a chain of conflicts in the history of man - conflicts between his ego and God. The conflict has appeared in different shapes. Under the garb of petty self or selfish interests, man's ego clouds his vision, and raises in him the urge to differentiate between one human being and another, and thus turns him away from the path of virtue. Religion comes in to prevent this process, furnishes a code of morals for man and serves as a fountainhead of truth such as can never dry up.

The portion of Mahābhārata's Bhīṣma Parva covering chapters 25 to 42 is called the Gītā. In these 18 chapters is recorded the conversation which took place between Srī Kṛṣṇa and Arjuna during the first stage of the war of Mahābhārata. On the tenth day of the war, it is stated Sañjaya related this conversation to Dhṛtarāṣtra. He said that he, by the kindness of Vyāsa, had heard it from the very mouth of Srī Kṛṣna himself

(18:75). It is written in the second chapter of Bhīṣma Parva that Vyāsa had bestowed upon Sañjaya the spiritual eye by which he, sitting away from the scene of war, could both see the battle and hear the conversation. Critics have doubted whether it was natural for Srī Kṛṣṇa and Arjuna to carry on such prolonged conversation of a serious nature when the contending armies were arrayed against each other, and whether it was ever possible for Sañjaya to see the battle ground from a far off region and hear the prolonged serious conversation between Srī Kṛṣṇa and Arjuna and remember all the ślōkas aright. The controversy that has raged over this was so acute that one critic has, out of seven hundred ślōkas, selected one hundred, a second critic thirty six, a third twenty eight and a fourth but seven as the ślōkas likely to have been uttered on the battle-field by Srī Kṛṣṇa and which later on were developed into seven hundred. As a way out, several scholars have offered the theory that the entire picture of the war is an allegory portraying the eternal conflict in the mind of man between good and evil.

In this connection one may agree with Lōkamānya Bāl Gangādhara Tilak where he says " those who are only interested in the spiritual aspect of the story, need not enter into any disputations over the outer form in which it is expressed. Whether the battle described in the Mahābhārata ever actually took place, whether Srī Kṛṣṇa and Arjuna ever held a conversation on the battle-field, whether Sañjaya was endowed with any inward eye or not, it is clear that the stanzas of the Gītā were composed neither by Srī Kṛṣṇa and Arjuna nor by Sañjaya. These were actually composed by Vyāsa. To regard the Gītā as having been expressed in the present form by Srī Kṛṣṇa and Arjuna, or on the other hand, to apply to it the canons of dialectics, does not seem to be an appropriate approach to the Gītā. In its own grand manner, and in keeping with the condition of life prevailing in the time of its composition, the Bhagavad Gītā, which is the essence of Upaniṣads and because of which we need not read other scriptures, presents to the perplexed souls of all times a beautiful and valuable message. (G. 18 : 79).

The Gītā refers to the various faiths which prevailed in its days, as well as to different religious thoughts, methods of worship, rites and rituals, superstitions and philosophic notions which were in vogue, and examines their validity. Laying stress on the basic common factor among the different faiths, viz., worship of one Īśwara, it strives to promote a sort of unity. It argues that self-control and righteousness form the first steps in the spiritual progress and are enjoined by every faith. It states that salvation lies in giving up the thought of discriminating between one's own self and another, or in tearing the veils of differentiations between one another, and in absorbing the entire world in one's own self and letting one's own self be absorbed in the entire world. The Gītā insists on seeing one Parameśwara in all things animate and inanimate. At the end, it points the way, through the purification of one's soul and the exercising of complete control over it, of passing from one lower stage to a higher stage. That indeed is the theme of the Bhagavad Gītā.

Now, have we to find where each of the several aspects of the Gītā's message leads us, and what lesson have we to derive from them?

To understand the Gītā, we have first of all to understand the conditions, thoughts, rites and rituals of the time of Gītā so far as the Gītā gives an account of them.

The difficult issue which, at the very beginning of the Gītā, Arjuna places before Srī Kṛṣna for consideration may briefly be stated. He says:

> "If I take part in this battle, our entire family will perish. With their destruction, will dissapper their ancient customs and rites and rituals that regulate their life (1 : 40). And when these disappear, there will remain nothing to offer guidance and serve as moral checks to those who survive, more particularly to the womanfolk among them. In consequence, corruption will prevail and women's morality will get undermined. (1 : 41). Once this happens, inter-mixture of castes will follow, and there will remain then no distinction between one caste and another. And when such an intermixture takes place, those that have caused the destruction

> of their families, as well as, those that survive, will go to Hell, Even their ancestors will go there, because there will be left no one of their progeny with racial purity qualified to perform the rites of food and water for the upkeep of their souls. As a result of the sins of the destroyers of the families, the traditional rites, rituals, and laws will be destroyed once for all. (1 : 43). We have been hearing from time immemorial that those whose rites and rituals are thus destroyed, Hell becomes their permanent abode (1 : 44). It will therefore be a heinous sin for us to take part in this battle."

Arjuna has used the word pāpa (sin) three times in this chapter (1: 39, 38, 45). The conception of sin which is in the mind of Arjuna is not what it ordinarily connotes viz., the killing of men in general. But it is the sin of killing one's own kith and kin or the destruction of one's clan itself (1: 38-39). We have to remember that by castes as mentioned in the Gītā (1: 43) we should not mean the usual castes, viz. Brāhmaṇas, Kṣatriyas, Vaiśyas, and Sūdras. In those days, the conception of caste differed from that of race. Both were recognised on the basis of birth. There were differrent families then. From a study of Mahābhārata, it is gathered that among separate castes there used to be inter-marriages. Geneological table was based only on the father's line.

From the other chapters we gather a view of other matters pertaining to the age. One of them was the belief in the Vēdas. People were obsessed with what was stated therein (2: 42). Belief in them was rooted in their minds. That was the case with Arjuna too (2: 53). Talks on the Vēdas used to be immensely appreciated (2: 42). People of the times believed that there was nothing superior to the Vēdas (2: 43). But what they had actually adopted from the Vēdas for guidance in life were nothing but external rites and rituals such as Yajña, havana, japa, tapas, puja path, dān etc. (1: 43; 2: 20, 22; 11: 48-53). (11: 48, 53; 20, 21-9). To get pleasure and comfort in life and to gratify their worldly desires constituted their main goal of life. Their highest aim was to secure the pleasures of Paradise and to raise themselves to the position of the most favoured in the Life Beyond (9: 20, 21; 2: 44-43). To them

Hell was the place of pain and Paradise the abode of pleasure and comfort. Yajña was of several kinds (4: 32). In addition to what was indicated in the three Vēdas, the Ṛg, the Sāma and the Yajur (9-17-20), most of the people followed separate Smṛtis. There used to be Smṛti Yajña, besides the Yajña sanctioned by the Vēdas (19: 16). During the course of the practice of Vēdic and Smṛti ceremonies, various kinds of maṅtrams were recited and 'Ghee' and different articles of food offered (9: 16, 4: 24) and the Soma juice drunk (9: 20). It is clear from the second, sixth, and ninth and the succeeding chapters that in those days people were concerned only with the external forms of religious rites and rituals. They had nothing to do with their high and universal principles which could prove useful to all men of all countries and nations alike.

People used to worship several deities besides one Paramēśwara. They used to invoke them for the fulfilment of their various desires. Worldly comforts formed objects of their appeals. Various attempts used to be made to please these deities. In their names, various objects used to be offered as sacrifices (3: 11-12; 4: 12-25; 7: 20-23). Flowers, leaves, fruits and water also formed the objects of their offerings (26-9). Besides deities, ghosts and devils used to be worshipped, and seperate sacrifices and offerings made to each.

The people of the times believed in omens too (1: 31). As in the case of the people of the four castes, viz. Brāhmaṇas, Kṣatriyas, Vaisyas and Sūdras, there were separate rites assigned to the Sanyāsis etc. Emphasis was laid on the external forms instead of internal purity. The Sanyāsis for example, were prohibited from touching fire and required to do or not to do this or that thing (1-6). Those who believed in one Paramēśwara pursued several ways to know or to approach Him (4:11). In short, there were various sects and faiths in the country during these days (18:66). Some people believed in miracles, and pursued two methods to attain them, one by making offerings and the other by practising asceticism in seclusion.

Under these conditions, it is but natural that from the philosophical point of view, two conflicting thoughts existed in the land to which constant reference is made in the Gītā (2: 3; 3: 3; 13: 24). The followers of the thought of Sānkhya Mārga laid emphasis on devotion instead of external observance of rites and rituals, and considered devotion the only way to attain salvation. They regarded every other work as evilsome and prohibitive (3: 18) and preferred family life to that of renunciation. The followers of another thought believed in the observance of rites and rituals which they believed led to salvation. The Gītā calls both these ways as Yōga (2: 3). In those days various forms of Prāṇāyāma (breath control) too were in vogue (4: 29; 13: 24).

It is plainly written in the Gītā that it was not only the time of agression of Kurus against Pandus, but it was also the period when religious faith was on the decline and disbelief on the increase. It was just the time for the appearance of Prophets, the delivery of holy books such as the Gītā and the return of real faith (7: 8-9).

Arjuna having fallen a victim to these false notions of faith, worship, and beliefs of his times, could not perceive the straight path to see the right thing. This is why Arjuna appealed to Srī Kṛṣṇa to lead him to the right path. Srī Kṛṣṇa's reply to Arjuna in this regard constitutes the Gītā Upadēśa.

We shall now take a cursory view of each of the several chapters of the Gītā separately. Here and there in these chapters some points have been repeated under different aspects, a is usual in books of religious injunctions.

THE RELIGION OF THE GĪTĀ

CHAPTER I

We have already referred to the considerations which weighed with Arjuna in his hesitation to fight the Kauravas- His pleading before Srī Kṛṣṇa was:

"On account of this war, our family and all the tradi, tions and rituals of our community will be destroyed. None will be left to perform the funeral rites. If our faith is thus destroyed, the entire family will go to Hell." He had further stated: "We have been hearing from our ancestors that whenever the old faith disappears, all the people are thrown into Hell." The first chapter of the Gīta is occupied with this pleading of Arjuna.

CHAPTER II

Srī Kṛṣṇa's reply begins with the second chapter. He tried to evade the solution of Arjuna's problems by blaming him for his inordinate devotion (2:2) to his family which he thought was the result of his weakness of heart, and was therefore unworthy of his high position (2:3). When Arjuna was not satisfied with this reply, Srī Kṛṣṇa said smiling:

"Arjuna! on the one hand, you talk like a wise man, and on the other, you nervously think of objects which no one should care for. It is not the work of a sensible man to ponder over who or what has been or what will be destroyed?" (2:11).

Srī Kṛṣṇa tries at first to dispell Arjuna's fears by telling him that they did not deserve to be entertained seriously.

Here the difference between Arjuna's and Srī Kṛṣṇa's conception of dharma or faith deserves serious attention. Arjuna conceives dharma as rituals and religious rites (1: 43), while Srī Kṛṣṇa regards it as service to others (2 : 31).

From the eleventh to the thirtieth stanza of the second chapter, Srī Kṛṣṇa, dealing with the philosophy of death, happiness and sorrow, says that the soul is immortal, while the body and all that is in the world, all names and forms, are transitory and perishable.

The Gītā says: "Some witness, some talk about, and some listen to the secrets of hfe with unconcealed amazement, but none of them understands them." (2: 29).

So far as the practical aspects of the philosophy of the Gītā are concerned, they are described in the very words of the Gītā itself.

"All the work which is done as a duty selflessly irrespective of any resultant happiness and pain, gain and loss, success and failure, is verily unattained and free of sin." (2 : 38). In other words, the root cause of sin lies in our ownself.

Having pointed this out, Srī Kṛṣṇa addresses Arjuna:

"Till now, I have been explaining to you from the intellectual point of view. Now, I shall explain the same thing from the practical point of view. If you comprehend this, you will realize fully what your duty is" (2 : 39).

It may be pointed out here that Arjuna has given expression to his views without specifically referring them to the Vēdas or to their teachings. On the other hand, Srī Kṛṣṇa bearing in mind the condition of his times and also the influence exerted by the Vēdas on the mind of Arjuna, deliberately refers to them, in so far as they were responsible in building up the mind of Arjuna. Says he to Arjuna:

"The teachings of the Vēdas have caused you the loss of your wisdom. Unless your wisdom returns to you, you cannot understand properly the real path of Karma Yōga (2 : 53). Those who find themselves pledged to the teachings of the Vēdas and assert that there is nothing superior to them, they are verily devoid of wisdom and are in pursuit of worldly desires. Such people want to enjoy the pleasures of Paradise and try to get bodily comforts by talking sweet things about the various outwards forms of religion, such as, rituals and rites by adhering to which they expect to get the pleasures and comforts of life. Their mind is given over to the enjoyment of pleasures and comforts. Their desires have undermined their wisdom. That is the reason why their minds have not gained equilibrium, and cannot concentrate on the performance of the actual duties of life. (2 : 42, 43, 44)

"The minds of such people, instead of getting channelised into one single purpose to discharge their duty as duty, uninfluenced by selfish interests, pursue desires which have no limit set to them. Hence their minds remain unsettled. (2 : 41).

"The teachings of the Vedas confine persons to three qualities, viz , Satva (contentment) Rajas (action) and Tamas (Laziness). You (Arjuna) should keep yourself above them, as well as, above pleasures and pain, and above differentiations of kith and kin and others. 'Satva' should be your watch word. Do not desire anything for personal gain, and do not get yourself attached to anything for pesonal ends. Concentrate your mind on the well-being of your soul. (2 : 45)

"To the Brāhmaṇa or the wise man who has understood Reality, the Vēdas are as useless as a small solitary well amidst extensive water-beds. (2 : 46).

By the Vēdas is meant what is stated therein about mere external forms of worship, rituals and religious rites. (9: 20–21).

After this, Srī Kṛṣṇa advised Arjuna to do his duty for the sake of duty selflessly, uninfluenced either by the thought of success or failure. He denounced the tendency to turnaway from duty, and declared proper service to others as real Yōga. (2 : 50).

On Srī Kṛṣṇa's remark that the mind turned aside from the right path by the external vēdic rituals and rites needs to be set right, Arjuna asks him how he should find out the man whose mind is steady and unwavering. The closing eighteen stanzas of the second chapter furnish Srī Kṛṣṇa's reply to Arjuna's query. They constitute the essence of the Gītā. Says Srī Kṛṣṇa:

"O Arjuna! He who can conquer the desires which are roused in his mind is neither afraid of pain nor is enamoured of pleasure. He who has no attachment with anything and is afraid of nothing and hates none, and keeps under control his desires, is the ideal man, the man with sound wisdom (balanced mind). One should hold together his desires under control, even as the turtle draws into its shell its head and feet (when afraid of any harm to itself). Despite the efforts to suppress one's desires, the mind now and then wavers. The only remedy in such cases lies in gradually directing such desires into the path of Īśwara. He, who neither loves nor hates anything that is worldly and effectively controls his senses, may do all kinds of worldly acts and yet achieve peace of mind and contentment. He who exercises self-control can easily avoid pleasure-loving people and can concentrate his mind on purifying his inner self and strengthening his soul. His real work consists in controlling his self. This is the only way to achieve real contentment and real comfort; to live with Īśwara and attain salvation. (2 : 55 to 72).

CHAPTER III

Again, Arjuna was confronted with another question. He asked himself why he should not renounce the world when he had to suppress his self in order to achieve salvation.

In reply to this query, an explanation has been offered in the third chapter as follows:

"He who renounces the world without discharging his worldly duties cannot attain perfection (3 : 4). His efforts for his personal ends, in entire disregard of his service to others and their welfare, will create for him a series of troubles. He should therefore discharge his duties unselfishly (3 : 9). It is such selfless work that has contributed to human welfare from the beginning of the world. The man who prepares food for himself alone, verily commits sin; and when he does not share it with others, he deserves to be called a thief (3: 12-13). This is what Yajña or service to others really means. One who indulges in his own selfish desires leads a mean life (3 : 16). Man should not think of getting his personal interests served by others (3: 18). He can reach Īśwara only through his selfless service to humanity (3 : 10). Service to others is the royal road to the attainment of perfection, and therein lies the good of all people (3 : 20). While thoughtless people are usually engrossed in efforts for personal ends, men of wisdom work for the welfare of others (3: 25). Keeping himself above hope and love, and putting his heart and soul into spiritual pursuit, man should perform his duties for the sake of Īśwara" (3 : 30).

"To man certain objects are attractive, and certain others are repulsive. He should strive to rise superior to this tension; for, it is the conflicting promptings of love and hate that are his enemies" (3 : 24).

"Whenever and wherever you have to discharge a duty, do it with a religious zest. Nothing should deviate you from it. It is good to die performing your duty." (3: 35).

"Two things lead man to evil. They are the twin enemies of man. One is sexual passion, the other is anger. Just as smoke conceals fire, and dust clouds the mirror, the two passions render man's mind unsound." (2: 37-38).

"It is therefore necessary first of all to control or suppress those passions which destroy the mind of man and his intellect." (3 : 41).

Senses are sufficiently pure; but mind is purer than senses, and intellect is purer than mind. The soul is the purest of all. The soul is everything and that is He (3 : 42).

"By understanding this, by overcoming these senses and by suppressing or inhibiting desires march on towards the soul (3: 42-43). This is the real faith, and this is the Yōga that has come down to us from of old: Negligence of this has misled people today and made them indulge in external rituals which do not really constitute faith." (3 : 1-4).

THE RELIGION OF THE GĪTĀ

CHAPTER IV

In the fourth chapter, it has been stated that whenever people forget this true faith and take false faiths as true and adopt them, great souls are born who once again show the path of true faith (4 : 7-8).

Those people who eliminate from their mind hatred, anger and fear, and seek Parmēśwara's help and concentrate their mind on Him, attain real wisdom and ultimately achieve union with Him (4 : 10).

To get salvation, rituals and rites are not needed. What is needed is the directing one's mind towards one Paramēśwara after eliminating from it hatred, fear and anger.

So far as external religious rites are concerned which one may call Shar'a or Karma Kāṇda, and which establish differences between one religion and another, the Bhagawad Gītā looks at them from one single angle and says:

In whatsoever way any come to Me,
In that same way I grant them favour.
My path follow
Men altogether, son of Pṛtha. (4 : 11)

Like those who, standing around a circle, start from various directions towards the central point, and ultimately reach their goal, so do those who follow different faiths ultimately reach One Paramēśwara.

The Gītā therefore opines :

" The wise man should in no case cross the path of those persons who, despite their lack of sound wisdom, are leading a righteous life, nor should he make them waver or create doubts in their mind about their own way of righteous life. Rather, he should keep them engaged in their own pursuit of righteous life." (3 : 26-29).

Referring to the system of four castes, viz. Brāhmaṇa, Kṣatria, Vaiśya and Śudra, the Gītā says that it is not for man to carve out such a system, nor should such a system rest on one's birth. God has created people with four diffrent attributes which manifest themselves in the selection of four different types of profession. This difference is natural, and one should therefore regard the different aptitudes as bases of Brāhmaṇa, Kṣatria and the rest (4 : 13).

In the succeeding chapter No. 18, are described the qualities which each of the several castes must possess in order to discharge satisfactorily the duties assigned to each (18: 41-44). The Gītā says that each man should select his profession according to his inclination or inherent qualities. It is then alone, that he can achieve perfection in his selected line and thus serve the purfose of Īśwara and attain salvation (18 : 45-47).

For instance, he who does his work without expecting any personal gain therefrom is verily a Pandit. His mind is under his control. He is free from the sense of otherness. He hates none. Whatever he does, he does it selflessly, for the sake of Īśwara and for improving the lot of his fellow men, and is free from personal attachment to all that is worldly (4: 19-23).

Whatever man does, he should do it with the conviction that whatever he sees in the world is the manifestation of Īśwara Himself, that truth is immortal and the rest is untrue and perishable, and that ultimately all would return to Him and merge in Him. To so discharge one's duties is true Yajña or devotion (3 : 23-24).

People indulge in various forms of Yōga such as asceticism (tapas) and breath-control (prāṇāyāma or habs-i-tham) as prescribed in ihe Vėdas, but real devotion is the attainment of knowledge of divine presence in man which if once attained, never lets one be deceived by any false devotion. True knowledge consists in seeing all sections of mankind within one's own self, and all objects within Īśwara and Īśwara within all objects (4 : 25-35). To look upon others even as one looks upon himself, and to see Īśwara in every one is to attain, as repeatedly pointed out by the Gītā, the utmost knowledg of God.

For man there is no knowledge higher than this which could purify man. The true Yōgi gradually discovers it within himself (4 : 38). For this purpose conviction and control of senses are essential (4 : 39).

CHAPTER V

In the fifth Chapter, Arjuna repeated the same question. He asked which one of the two ways is better, the way of the recluse who depends upon his own wisdom for his guidance, or that of the one who performs all worldly duties and strives to seek the welfare of his soul.

In reply to the above, the Gītā states that both the paths adopted by them are in essence one and the same, and it therefore tries to reconcile the one with the other.

Says Srī Kṛṣṇa :

"Those who regard Sāṅkhya Mārga and Karma Mārga as two separate ways, are mere children. Pandits or men of wisdom do not consider the two ways as separate from each other. By following any one of these paths properly, every man can reap the desired reward, and reach the same destination. One who regards both the ways as one is in the right (5: 4-5).

Proceeding Srī Kṛṣṇa says :

That man is true Sanyāsi who hates none, and desires nothing, who keeps himself above the sense of otherness, who is engaged in discharging his duty, whose mind is pure, who has control over his self, whose senses are under his command who looks upon the soul of every one as if it is his own, who does every work for the sake of Īśwara without any personal aim or attachment and who in this way purifies his soul (5: 3-11).

Those who in this way discharge their duties with understanding illuminate their inner self and seek Paramēśwara within. They then attain salvation by attaching themselves to Him and wash their sins (5 : 15-17).

> In a knowledge–and cultivation-perfected
> Brahman, a cow, an elephant,
> And in a mere dog, and an outcaste,
> The wise see the same thing. (18 : 18)

The true Pandit is he who makes no difference between a learned and a humble Brāhmaṇa, a cow, an elephant, a dog and a wretch (5 : 18).

Those who possess such a conviction in the unity of all creations conquer all that is in the world, because Parmēśwara is equally manifest in every thing, which in other words is the manifestation of Paramēśwara Himself (5: 19).

The pleasure of the senses ultimately results in pains. The wise do not adore them. He who during his life time and before his death can attain control over his self and passions, he alone will be regarded as a real Yōgi, a man with peace of mind and contentment. He who finds within his own soul peace, contentment and light, gets salvation by merging himself in Paramēśwara. Salvation is attained by those who find themselves and who have kept themselves always busy in their service to others (5 : 22-26).

In the three stanzas that follow, the process of progress beyond this Ātma is described. It is written:

> Putting out outside contacts,
> And fixing the sight between the eye-brows,
> Making even the upper and nether breaths,
> As they pass thro the nose;
> Controlling the senses, thought-organ, and intelligence,
> The sage bent on final release,
> Whose desire, fear, and wrath are departed —
> Who is ever thus, is already released.
> The Recipient of worship and austerities,
> The Great Lord of the whole world,
> The Friend of all beings —
> Me knowing, he goes to peace. (5 : 27-29)

CHAPTER VI

Sāṅkhya and Karma being shown once again as one, the Gīta states:

He who does not mind the results of his efforts and he who discharges conscientiously what he thinks to be his duty, such a man is a sanyāsi, as well as, a Yōgi. The sanyāsi who lays stress on the performance of external rites such as refusing to touch fire, and doing or not doing this or that kind of work, is no sanyāsi at all (6 : 1-2). Sanyās is the name given to a state of mind, and is not a name for external rituals or a particular way of dress.

For the man who wants to attain Yōga, his path lies in his performance of his worldly duties. Once he achieves it, he finds within himself that peace of mind and energy which serve as incentives to the performance of all his duties (6 : 3).

Man is his own friend, as well as, his own enemy. He who has conquered his self is his own friend, and he who has allowed his self to conquer him is his enemy (6 : 5-6)

He who has conquered his self, maintains peace of mind, and he who is in no way affected by cold or heat, pleasure or pain, his Ātma becomes Paramātma (6 : 7).

He who makes no difference between friend and foe, between his own people and others, is the right man (6 : 9).

After this, the Gītā describes certain ways of performing Yōga:

Let the disciplined man ever discipline
    Himself, abiding in a secret place,
Solitary, restraining his thoughts and soul,
    Free from aspirations and without possessions
In a clean place establishing
    A steady seat for himself,
That is neither too high nor too low,
    Covered with a cloth, a skin, and kuśa-grass,
There fixing the thought-organ on a single object,
    Restraining the activity of his mind and senses,
Sitting on the seat, let him practise
    Discipline unto self-purification.
Even body, head, and neck
    Holding motionless, (keeping himself) steady,
Gazing at the tip of his own nose,
    And not looking in any direction,
With tranquil soul, rid of fear,
    Abiding in the vow of chastity,
Controlling the mind, his thoughts on Me,
    Let him sit disciplined, absorbed in Me. (6 : 10-14)
Thus ever disciplining himself,
    The man of discipline, with controlled mind,

To peace of that culminates in nirvāṇa,
    And rests in Me, attains. (6 : 15)

And which having gained, other gain
    He counts none higher than it;
In which established, by no misery,
    However grievous, is he moved. (6 : 22)

The Gītā stresses that this Yōga is intended neither for those who are attached to the world, nor for those who shirk worldly duties.

He alone can remove worldly pain who maintains balance in his living condition, in his food, drink, and residence, sleep and work, and takes the middle course in discharging his duties (6 : 17).

From the 18th to the 28th stanzas, the same thing has been described in detail with the ultimate aim or purpose of getting one's soul merged in God, or become 'Fana-filla' 'lost in God', as termed by the Sūfis.

It has been said again :

Himself as in all beings,
    And all beings in himself,
Sees he whose self is disciplined in discipline,
    Who sees the same in all things,

Who sees Me in all,
    And sees all in Me,
For him I am not lost,
    And he is not lost for Me.

Me as abiding in all beings whoso
    Reveres, adopting (the belief in) one-ness,
Tho abiding in any possible condition,
    That disciplined man abides in Me.

By comparison with himself, in all (beings)
    Whoso sees the same, Arjuna,
Whether it be pleasure or pain,
    He is deemed the supreme disciplined man. (6 : 29-32)

To this, said Arjuna that it was difficult to control the wavering human mind. And Srī Kṛṣṇa replied:

"For this, studied detachment from worldly things is necessary" (6 : 35). "He who has no control over himself, he cannot attain this Yōga" (6 : 39). "The External rites and rituals do not prove helpful to him, because the man in whom the desire for Yōga pulsates, needs neither Vēdas nor their rites and rituals, and he rises above all these" (6 : 44). "And when he makes at least some effort in this direction, even though his mind wavers, and he does not attain complete success, his efforts, however feeble, will not prove futile, nor will his life beyond this world be in any way adversely affected; its progress will rather continue there. This way is much better than 'Tap or asceticism', 'Jñana or gnosis' and 'Karma Kāṇḍa or religious law' (6 : 37-46).

CHAPTER VII

To those who want to know Paramēśwara, it has been shown in the Seventh chapter that He is found everywhere and in each and everything. It has been also indicated what difference lies between Paramēśwara and demi-gods. Stress is laid in this chapter on the worship of One God, Paramēśwara or Allāh.

There are two aspects of Paramēśwara's powers. On their account the entire world — all the creatures that have taken their birth — Earth, water, fire, air, ether, mind, wisdom and self are all Īśwara's manifestations. All life that pulsates in these creatures indicates the hidden source of Īśwara. Īśwara alone is both creator and destroyer of the world. All things in the world are so related to each other within Him as are several beads in a necklace. Īśwara Himself is the essence of all. He constitutes life-giving quality in water, light in the moon and the sun, 'Ōm' in the Vēdās, sound in the atmosphere, courage in men, fragrance in soil, glow in fire, endurance in the ascetic. He is the life of all living things. He is the wisdom of the wise, the majesty of the ascetic, and the strength of the strong. He is free from sex and other passions. Although He is the creator of the strands, the source of tranquility, and action and laziness, He transcends them all. Obsessed by these, the world cannot recognize or understand Him. He is immortal and is different from them (7 : 4-13).

In the pursuit of minor desires, some people senselessly worship demi-gods. In whomsoever they believe, Paramēśwara strengthens their belief. Whatever results they may achieve thereby, it is Paramēśwara Himself who has fixed them. But the fruits obtained by these senseless people are perishable. Those who worship demi-gods ultimately reach them and those who worship One Paramēśwara, on the other hand, reach Paramēśwara Himself. The thing is that those who are devoid of wisdom and do not understand Paramēśwara in His Reality, want to worship Him in some visible form. In a way the forms given to demi-gods are the forms of objects created by Paramēśwara Himself; but Paramēśwara is formless and has had no birth; He neither grows nor decays, is free from the process of life and death, and He is immortal and above everything else. People who lack in wisdom cannot comprehend Him. He has full knowledge of the past, the present and the future. He who rises superior to love and hate, and the sense of otherness in relation to fellow creatures, commits no sins, does righteous acts and worships only One Paramēśwara — he alone can understand Reality and attain salvation (7 : 20-30).

CHAPTER VIII

It is necessary for man to think of the one Paramēśwara when he has to drop his body or to die. It is then only that he can reach Him. Those who think at that time of other deities or of worldly interests, have in their minds nothing but petty thoughts. While performing one's duties in this world, one should always continue to pray to One Paramēśwara. He is everything, is All-Knowing, Immortal, Controller and sustainer. No eye can see Him and no ear can hear Him. No vision can comprehend Him. He is beyond darkness, and He is light and nothing but light. Those who have studied Vēdas know Him to be eternal. He has neither a beginning, nor an end. All living things are within Him and He permeates everything. It is Paramēśwara of such a vision that one should worship. This path is much superior to and higher than what has been presented by the Vēdas through external rites and rituals. (8: 5, 6, 7, 9,10, 11, 22, 28).

In the intervening stanzas, it has been indicated how at the time of death man should focus his thoughts on Paramēśwara and what kind of thoughts should he have in his mind. In some of the stanzas, it has been shown how when one under certain conditions has to pass through dark paths entangles himself in the meshes of Swarga and Naraka (Paradise and Hell), and how when he dies under other conditions one passess through well-lighted paths and attains deserved salvation. These stanzas from 24 to 27 which describe the various conditions under which one dies are believed to be the most difficult sections of the Gītā. Scholars of the Gītā have tried to catch the meaning of these stanzas in various ways. Lōkamānya Tilak, while appreciating the opinion of past scholars, observes that those who adhere to the Vēdic rites and rituals and die, they pass through dark paths and get enmeshed in Swarga and Naraka. He says that he who rises superior to external rites, makes no discrimination between living things, and renders selfless service to one and all without any personal motive, or attachment, and then dies, he will pass through well-lighted paths and attain salvation (295-298 Gītā Rahasya).

CHAPTER IX

In the beginning of the ninth chapter, it is said that the secret of ultimate Reality is that he alone can comprehend who hates none. And it is only such a man that can sustain Dharma in his life.

Further it is written :
By Me is pervaded all this
Universe, by Me in the form of the unmanifest
All beings rest in Me,
And I do not rest in them. (9: 4)

As constantly abides in the ether
The great wind, that penetrates everywhere,
So all beings,
Abide in Me ; make sure of that. (9: 6)

Those who adore Paramēśwara with wisdom, perceive unity in multiplicity, and multiplicity in unity. Whichever side they cast their sight, verily they see His face. In all faiths and rites and rituals, they feel only His existence. He is the sacrifice in the sacrificial rite, and He is the fire, and He is the spell (mantram). He is the nectar, He the clarified butter. He is the oblation and the flames into which it is offered. He is the father of the Universe. He the mother; He, the Sustainer. He the grand sire of the Universe, He the 'ŌṀKĀR'. He the Ṛg Vēda, Sāma Vēda, and the Yajur Vēda. He is the Energy, He the Providence, He the master, He the Seer. He is the Resting Place for one and all, He the refuge, He the well-wisher of all. He the Creator, He the destroyer, He the Beginning, He the Middle and He the end. He is the seed of all — the seed that never perisheth. He it is who in the form of the sun burns. He it is who holds back the rain; and He it is who causeth rain (9 : 15-19).

Those people who observe scrupulously the rites and rituals of Vēdas seeking Paradise and celestial pleasures, they reap the fruits of their efforts that do not last long (9 : 20-21).

Those people who worship deities with sincerity, even they, in a way adore Paramēśwara Himself, though not in the enjoined fashion. All forms represent His Form. But the path these people have chosen is by no means the right path. They do not understand Paramēśwara properly. That is why they ultimately fall or return to the earth as mortals by being reborn. Before whatever form one bows his head in worship, he goes to that form only. If he worships demi-gods, he gets demi-gods; if he worships idols, he gets idols; if he worships human beings, he gets human beings; if he worships One Paramēśwara, he gets One Paramēśwara. Flowers, herbs, fruits or water - whatever is presented as offering — is accepted by Paramēśwara with the same amount of sincerity as that of the true devotee.

This is the reason why the Gītā says:

Whatever thou doest, whatever thou eatest,
    Whatever thou offerest in oblation or givest,
Whatever austerity thou performest, son of Kunti,
    That do as an offering to me. (9: 27)

Thus from what have good and evil fruits
    Thou shalt be freed (namely) from the bonds of action,
Thy soul disciplined in the discipline of renunciation,
    Freed, thou shalt go to Me.

I am the same to all beings,
    No one is hateful or dear to Me;
But those who revere Me with devotion,
    They are in Me and I too am in them.

Be Me-minded, devoted to me,
    Worship Me, pay homage to Me;
Just to Me shalt thou go,having thus disciplined
    Thyself, fully intent on Me (9:27, 28, 29 & 34)

Various kinds of rites and rituals, ways of worship, take their origin in the name of Paramēśwara. All the human forms i. e. forms put on by deities represent His form. From this point of view all these ways of devotion are sincere. But they are of course not the right ways. One who is wise enough abandons all such methods of devotion and adores only one Paramēśwara. Paramēśwara exists in all and constitutes their life-spring. If you set your heart upon Him, turning away from all desires, do your duties to others, and bow down to Him in self surrender, and discover Him in all his creation, you will soon come into His Being.

CHAPTER X

In the tenth and eleventh chapters an attempt has been made to give an idea of Paramēśwara who is Reality, before whom everything else is unreal, who is free from the limitations of personality, and personal individuality, who is above duality and separatism, who is beyond human vision, who pervades the entire universe, who is intelligible only through his countless manifestations and who is all-embracing.

Paramēśwara was not born and has no beginning. He is the Lord of the worlds. The Seers and Dēvas owe their origin to Him. Human families who have developed into communities and nations are the product of His thought. Even the passing thoughts in human minds take their origin from Him. He is the creator of the entire world. Men of wisdom, who adore Him, always discourse about Him, try to understand Him among themselves and try to enlighten one another, and thus secure bliss and contentment.

> With thoughts on Me, with life concentrated on Me,
> Enlightening one another,
> And telling constantly of Me,
> They find contentment and joy.

It is such people alone that attain right thinking and ultimately approach Paramēśwara.

Paramēśwara alone knows what he really is, but man can perceive Him only through His manifestations. His manifestations are countless; but some of them may be cited here in the very words of the Gītā. Says Srī Kṛṣṇa to Arjuna :

> Come then, I shall tell thee —
> Since My supernal-manifestations are marvellous —
> Regarding the chief ones, best of Kurus;
> There is no end to My extent. (10 : 19)
>
> I am the soul, Guḍākeśa,
> That abides in the heart of all beings;
> I am the beginning and the middle
> Of beings, and the very end too. (10 : 20)
>
> Of the Ādityas I am Viṣṇu
> Of lights the radiant sun,
> Of Maruts I am (their chief) Marīci,
> Of stars I am the moon. (10 : 21)
>
> Of Vēdas I am the Sāma Vēda.
> Of gods I am Vāsava (Indra),
> Of sense-organs I am the thought-organ,
> Of beings I am the intellect. (10 : 22)
>
> And of Rudras I am Śamkara (Śiva),
> Of sprites and orges I am the Lord of Wealth (Kubēra)
> Of (the eight) Vasus I am the Fire (god),
> Of mountain-peaks I am Mēru. (10 : 23)

Of house-priests the chief am I,
Bṛhaspati (the priest-god), know thou, son of Pṛthā;
Of army-lords, I am Skanda (god of war),
Of bodies of water I am the ocean. (10 : 24)
Of great sages I am Bhṛgu,
Of utterances I am the one syllable (Ōṁ),
Of acts of worship I am the muttered worship,
Of mountain-ranges Himālaya. (10 : 25)
The holy fig-tree of all trees,
Of devine sages Nārada,
Of gandharvas (heavenly musicians), Citraratha (their chief)
Of perfected beings, the seer Kapila. (10 : 26)
Uccaiḥśravas (Indra's steed) of horses,
Sprung from the nectar (churned out of ocean) know Me to be;
Of princely elephants, Airāvata (Indra's elephant)
And of men, the king. (10 : 27)
Of weapons I am (Indra's) vajra,
Of cows I am the Cow-of-Wishes,
I am the generating Kandarpa (god of love),
Of serpents I am (the serpent-king) Vāsuki. (10 : 28)
And I am Ananta of the Nāgas (fabulous serpents),
I am Varuṇa (god of water of water-creatures,)
Of departed fathers I am (their chief god) Aryaman,
I am Yama (god of death) of subduers. (10 : 29)
Of demons I am (their prince) Prahlāda,
I am time of impellent-forces,
Of beasts I am the King of beasts
I am the son of Vinatā (Garuḍa, Viṣṇu's bird) of birds. (10 : 30)
I am the wind of purifiers,
Rāma of warriors,
I am the dolphin of water-monsters,
Of rivers I am the Ganges. (10 : 31)
Of creations the beginning and the end,
And the middle too am I, Arjuna;
Of knowledges the knowledge of the over-soul,
I am speech of them that speak. (10 : 32)
Of syllables (letters) I am the letter A,
And the dvandva of compounds,
None but I am immortal Time,
I am the ordainer (Creator with faces in all directions.) (10 : 33)

I am death that carries off all,
And the origin of things that are to be;
Of feminine entities I am Fame, Fortune, Speech,
Memory, Wisdsm, Steadfastness, Patience. (10 : 34)

Likewise of chants the Great Chant,
The Gāyatri am I of meters,
Of months, (the first month) Mārgaśīrṣa am I,
Of seasons the flower-bearer (spring). (10 : 35)

I am gambling of rogues.
I am majesty of the majestic,
I am conquest, I am the spirit-of-adventure,
I am courage of the courageous. (10 : 36)

Of the Vṛṣṇi-clansmen I am Vāsudēva,
Of the sons of Pāṇḍu, Dhanaṁjaya (Arjuna)
Of hermits also I am Vyāsa,
Of sages the sage Uśanas. (10 : 37)

I am the rod (punitive force) of stern controllers,
I am statecraft of them that seek political success;
Taciturnity too am I of secret things,
I am knowledge of the knowing. (10 : 38)

Moreover whatsoever of all beings
Is the seed, that am I, Arjuna;
There is none such as could be without
Me, no being moving or unmoving. (10 : 39)

There is no end to my marvellous
Supernal-manifestations, scorcher of the foe;
But I have now declared by way of examples
The extent of my supernal-manifestation. (10 : 40)

Whatever being shows supernal-manifestations,
Or majesty or vigor,
Be thou assured that that in every case
Is sprung from a fraction of my glory. (10 : 41)

After all, this extensive
Instruction - what boots it thee, Arjuna?
I support this entire
World with a single fraction (of Myself), and remain so.
(10 : 42)

So, whatever being shows supernal manifestation or majesty or vigour is to be regarded as having sprung from a fraction of Divine glory. From this point of view all leaders of communities, all prophets, and saints are the manifestations of Divine glory. In fact, the entire world is supported by just a single fraction of that glory (10 : 42)

Paramēśwara is beyond human vision, and is free from any colour or form. Yet, He pervades all things in the Universe. Therefore, he who realizcs his own self can realize His creator.

The theme of this chapter is therefore styled at the beginning of the following eleventh chapter as the spiritual content of the Gītā.

CHAPTER XI

After this discourse, and by the grace of Srī Kṛṣna, the Master of Yōga, the ignorance of Arjuna was dispelled and he than beheld the super-form of Paramēśwara with the eyes of wisdom. He says: Paramēśwara has a thousand and varied forms. The entire world with all things animate and inert are seen in Him and His face is turned towards all directions. The collective light of a thousand suns is not comparable to His.

In Him the leaders of Aryans and non-Aryans, all the deities and prophets, can be seen. He possesses many faces, stomachs and eyes, as well as, many forms, and in fact all the forms in the Universe are on the model of His Divine form. In other words, He is found everywhere. He has no beginning and no end. His is the divine form from which emanate all forms. His light is spread in all the four directions. The sun and the moon constitute His eyes. His power is boundless. It extends from earth to heaven and all over the ten oceans. All are overawed by Him. All the creatures praise Him. He is eternal. He is the preserver of all faiths. As all the rivers ultimately join the ocean, so all creatures ultimately unite with Him. He is above space and time. He alone is death. The rest is the apparent cause of death. He is immortal and manifest. He is neither confined to space nor is He definable. He is above definition. He is the knower and the known. He is the water and He is the fire. He is Chandraman and He is Prajāpati. A thousand salutations to Him, over and over again and from all directions! He is fathomless and He is all courage. Though He holds in Him all that is in the Universe, He is by Himself a complete whole. He is the father of all, the adored of all, and the Highest. There is none like Him, and is Himself. In the shape of man, He is friend of all and loved by all (11 : 8-43).

Neither through sacrifice, nor the study of Vēdas, nor through strict austarities, alms and rituals, can His form be seen by mortals, except by a man who has full control over his self, and who is free from the sense of duality, and who alone therefore can ultimately unite with Paramēśwara (11 : 48, 53 and 54).

His best and loveliest form is that of man through which peace and contentment can be attained (11 : 51). He exists in all forms. His human form is the super-form. Therefore, whatever man does, he should do for His sake; and regard Him as the goal of all his efforts. Him alone he should worship. Having control over his own self, he should keep himself free from personal love and hatred, and be friendly with all human beings. Such a man alone can approach God (11 : 55).

CHAPTER XII

In the XII Chapter which is captioned as BHAKTI YŌGA, Arjuna once more took up the question whether the devotee who worships Paramēśwara's attributes represented by various deities is better than that man who adores Him in His Absolute state of the imperishable unmanifest. The Gītā's reply to Arjuna's question is as follows:

Those who worship Bhagawan's qualities with full concentration are to be regarded as the most disciplined.

As for those others, who revere Bhagawan, the unmanifest, undefinable, imperishable, unthinkable, omnipresent, unchanging and approach Him, with all the senses in check, are tranquil-minded, devoted to the welfare of humanity, and see the

Ātma in every creature (12 : 2, 3, 4), their task is more arduous, because the unmanifest goal is very difficult to attain by embodied souls (12 : 5).

The devotees therefore should keep themselves absorbed, leaving the results of devotion to Īśwara (12 : 6).

One who hates none, is friendly and compassionate to all, is free from the delusion of 'I', 'Mine', and 'Thine', is selfless, is unmoved both by pleasure and pain, is forgiving, ever contended, self-controlled, maintains unshakeable resolve, is dedicated to Īśwara in intellect and in mind — such a devotee is dear to Him (12 : 13, 14).

He who fears none in this world, and is unaffected either by pleasure of grief is dear to Īśwara (12 : 15).

He who is contended under all conditions, is free from the delusion of 'I' and 'Mine' and finds himself above pain and pleasure, and unmindful of the fruits of every action, he is dear to Īśwara (12 : 16).

He who neither delights nor loathes, neither grieves nor craves, renounces good and evil objects, and is full of devotion, he is dear to Īśwara (12 : 17).

He whose attitude is the same towards friend and foe, who is indifferent to honour and disgrace, heat and cold, pleasure and pain, who is free from attachment, who values praise and blame equally, who can control his speech, who is content with anything that comes, whose home is everywhere and nowhere, whose mind is steadfast and who is full of devotion is dear to Īśwara (12 : 19). But those who in implicit faith and intent on Īśwara, revere the nector of duty as has been declared here, are beyond measure dear to Īśwara (12 : 20).

CHAPTER XIII

The thirteenth chapter of the Gītā is most philosophical in its treatment. The name of Vēdānta Śaśtra (Brahma Sūtra) appears in Gītā only once and it is in this chapter alone that it is mentioned. What are the things that need to be known besides Ātma? Or, what is the field of Jñana or gnosis, and what is Ātma which comprehends everything? What is the way to gain true gnosis? What is it that is to be really known. And what is true gnosis or the rigt vision? An answer to each of these questionings is furnished in this chapter.

Broadly speaking, the human body is called the Field, because man sows seeds of action in it, and reaps their fruits. It consists of various elements, viz., the five senses of sound, sight, smell, touch and taste; also intellect, ego, earth, water, ether, air, and fire; man's ten organs of knowing and doing, mind consciousness and resolution; hatred and desire, pain and pleasure. These are so provided in the body that they act and react upon one another; and they are to be known and understood. But the life that pulsates in all these objects of the body does not alter, and is the knower and is its master, the Paramātma and Parama Puruṣa, transcendent and eternal (13 : 1, 2, 5, 6 & 22). It is on account of the relations existing between the knower and the known that the world has been formed. (13 : 26).

The royal road to true Jñana is this:

Be humble and harmless. Be upright and for-bearing. Serve your teacher with all the obedience at your command. Keep your mind and body clean. Be tranquil, steadfast and master your ego. Keep aloof from things that concern your senses. Free yourself from yourself. Beware of your mortal nature, its weakness, its subjection to birth, age, suffering and death. Be slave to nothing: wife, home or household; do not let your mind be distracted. Remain uninfluenced both by pain and pleasure. Adore Paramēśwara with undisturbed heart. Now and then, seek solitude and avoid crowd, its noise and its fruitless commotion. Strive without ceasing to know the Ātma. Seek its knowledge and clearly comprehend why you should seek it. Here lie the roots of the true wisdom. All else is mere ignorance (13 : 7, 11).

What is it that one should know most of all things? It is Parabrahma who has no beginning. Everywhere are His hands, eyes and feet, His heads and His faces. He exists encompassing all things. Yet He is above or separate from them. He does the task of each of the senses. He hates none and protects all. Himself devoid of attributes, He constitutes the centre of all attributes. He is both within and without all the animate objects. He is subtle beyond the grasp of human mind. He is near and yet distant. He seems to divide Himself into objects and creatures, and yet He exists in them undivided. He is the sustainer of all, and also destroyer, and munifests Himself in all forms. Light of all Lights, He abides away from darkness. He is the dweller of all hearts and is both the knower and the knowledge (13 : 12-17).

Dhyan (meditation), Jñana (gnosis) and Karma (action) are the three ways to comprehend Him (13 : 24).

The vision of that man alone is true who sees Him exist in all things alike, who in view of the presence of God in all things does not cause harm to any one. It is such a man that attains perfection. When man perceives one and the only God in all His creations, He is said to have comprehended properly that Purṇa Brahma and that Paramātma who is devoid of attributes and who is unchanging. Like the air which is spotless despite the fact that it compasses all objects, Ātma remains spotless despite its existence in all creations. Even as the sun gives its light to the world, the Ātma illuminates it (13 : 27-33).

CHAPTER XIV

In this Chapter a description is given of three Guṇas (Attributes) — Sattwa (peace), Rajas (motion), and Tamas (laziness).

Sattwa, Rajas and Tamas take their origin from Prakṛti (matter). These three bind the soul to the body.

Among these, 'Sattwa' is pure, clean, and bright. It offers the soul happiness and knowledge. 'Rajas' is the outcome of passion and desire, and constitutes the main source of action. 'Tamas' is born of darkness and entraps you in ignorance, sluggishness and slumber. A tug of war goes on among these three. Whichever of the three guṇas is dominant at the time of your death, you reap the fruits thereof in your future life. Àtma or Paramātma is above these three guṇas. When man therefore succeeds in keeping himself above these guṇas, he becomes 'guṇātīta' and attains salvation (14 : 5-20).

The state of guṇatīta is that where man is indiffrent to the light of Sattwa, or the activity of Rajas, or the delusion of the tamas. Such a man does not either subject himself to sluggishness or get his mind distracted or disturbed by these three. Like the 'udāsīna', the disinterested, he looks upon everything, joy and pain, with an equal eye. Earth and stone, gold and silver are of equal value to him. He knows no difference between one kind of taste and another. Praise and blame, honour and disgrace are alike to him. Friend and foe are to him one and the same. He who finds himself above all desires, he gets over all strands, and worships God with unfaltering love, becomes 'guṇātīta' and attains 'Sādharmya' or gets absorbed in God who is the store house of life, contentment and eternal bliss (14 : 22-27).

CHAPTER XV

In this chapter the world is compared to the pipal tree.

With roots aloft and branches below
The eternal pipal-tree, they say—
Whose leaves are the (Vēdic) hymns,
Who knows it he knows the Vēda. (15 : 1)

Below and upward extend its branches,
Nourished by the strands, with the objects of sense as sprouts;
Below also are stretched forth its roots,
Resulting in actions, in the world of men. (15 : 2)

Its form is not thus comprehended here in the world,
Nor its end nor beginning nor basis,
This pipal-tree, with its firmly grown roots,
Cutting with the stout axe of detachment. (15 : 3)

Then that place must be sought
To which having gone men no more return,

(Thinking) 'I take refuge in that same primal spirit,
Whence issued forth of old the (whole cosmic) activity
(16:4)

Those sages who have suppressed their self, who have no attachment with worldly things, who are busy with their practicc of spiritual discipline, who entertain no desires. who rise superior to the sense of duality and who are not affected by either pain or pleasure — it is they who attain the station or go to the place where neither the sun, nor the moon shine, nor the fire glows, and from where no one returns (15 : 5, 6)

The soul is the manifestation of Īśwara. Deluded by mind and senses, it is caught by the wheel of mundane life (15 : 7).

The supreme source of everything is Īśwara Himself. His enargy enters the earth sustaining all that lives thereon. Through the moon, he gives sap and moisture to plants. He provides food and energy to all creatures. He alone abides in the hearts of all, and from whom knowledge, memory, etc. take their rise. The Yōgis behold Him in their own consciousness. He is the knower, and He alone knows everything. He who knows Him also knows everything (15 : 11-15) (15 : 18-19)

CAAPTER XVI

This chapter classifies men under two different qualities, viz. Daivi sampat (the divine) and Āsuri sampat (the demoniac). The divine lot leads to the release of the soul, and the demoniac to bondage.

The 'Daivi sampat' possesses twenty six virtues The man who belongs to this category, (1) is afraid of nothing, (2) is pure at heart, (3) perseveres in his march towards his union with God, (4) is charitable, (5) exercises control over the senses, (6) strives for the welfare of others, (7) reads good things, (8) practises austerity, (9) hates none and harms none, (10) practises spiritual discipline, (11) is truthful, (12) does not get angry, (13) renounces the things of the world, (14) has a tranquil mind (15) possesses no malicious tongue, (16) is compassionate to all, (17) avoids greed, (18) is gentle, (19) is modest, (20) abstains from useless activity, (21) has faith in the strength of his higher nature, (22) forgives, (23) endures, (24) is clean in thought and action, (25) entertains no enmity to any, and (26) is not proud (16 : 1-3).

Āsuri Sampat or the man of demoniac nature on the other hand, (1) maintains pretentions, (2) is proud, (3) conceited, (4) wrathful, (5) cruel, and (6) ignorant (16 : 4).

The thirteen stanzas that follow describe the mode of life of men of Āsuri sampat type. Such men greatly resemble the leaders of the present day advanced nations, and of other nations who have come under their influence. The picture raised is so true to life that a literal translation of these thirteen stanzas is given below:

Both activity and its cessation
Demoniac folk know not;
Neither purity nor yet good conduct
Nor truth is found in them. (16 : 7)

Without truth, without religious basis, they
Say is the world, without a God,
Not originating in regular mutual causation;
In short, motivated by desire alone. (16 : 8)

Holding fast to this view,
Men of lost souls, of scant intelligence,
Spring up, committing cruel deeds,
Unto the ruin of the world, noxious folk. (16 : 9)

Clinging to insatiable desire,
Filled with hopocrisy, arrogance, and pride,
Thro delusion taking up false notions,
They proceed with unclean undertakings. (16 : 10)

To limitless care,
That lasts until death, they are devoted;
They make the enjoyment of desires their highest aim,
Convinced that that is all; (16 : 11)

Bound by hundreds of bonds of longing,
Devoted to desire and wrath,
In order to enjoy desires, they seek
Hoardings of wealth by wrong means. (16 : 12)

"This have I gained today,
This desire I shall get,

Mine is this, and mine also this
Wealth again is going to be; (16:13)
Yonder enemy has been slain by me,
And I shall slay others too;
I am lord, I control enjoyments,
I am successful, mighty, happy; (16:14)
'I am rich, of noble birth;
Who else is like unto me?
I shall sacrifice and give gifts, and rejoice!'
Thus they say, deluded by ignorance. (16:15)
Led astray by many fancies,
Enveloped by the snares of delusion,
Intent on the enjoyment of desires,
They fall to a foul hell. (16:16)
Self-conceited, haughty,
Full of pride and arrogance of wealth
They do acts of religious worship in name alone,
Hyprocritically, not according to the (Vedic) injunctions. (16:17)
Egotism, force, pride,
Desire, and wrath they have taken to,
Me in their own and others' bodies
Hating, these envious men. (16:18)
These cruel and hateful
Base men, in the ceaseless round of existences,
These wicksd ones, I ccnstantly hurl
Into demoniac wombs alone. (16:19)

Their end is surely bad. They get away from truth and reality, and sink down to the lowest possible condition of the soul (16 : 20).

This is of hell the threefold
Gate, and ruins the soul:
Desire, wrath, and greed,
Hence one should abandon these three. (16:21).

Hell has three doors : lust, wrath and greed. They open for man's ruin. He must therefore avoid them all. He who avoids the three dark doors, achieves his salvation. It is necessary that man should make the eternal moral law of life his guide. He should scrupulously follow it and avoid to pursue his carnal desires. (16 : 21, 24).

CHAPTER XVII

In this chapter, Arjuna once more puts a question:

What do you think of those persons who offer sacrifices to God in accordance with their own personal conviction without following the instructions of the scriptures? (17 : 1)

Srī Kṛṣṇa replies :

Faith among human beings, is of three kinds. It springs from their very nature. It is characterised by goodness, or passion or darkness, according to man's dominant tendencies. (17 : 2)

> In accord with the essential nature of every man
> Is his faith, son of Bharata!
> Man here is made up of faith;
> As a man's faith is, Just so is he. (17 : 3)

The men of demoniac nature mortify their bodies impelled by egotism and vanity. Their austerities are thus demoniac (Āsuri). In their foolishness, they weaken alltheir sense organs, and God who dwells in their bodies does not approve of their austerities (17 : 5, 6).

Man's eating and drinking, his sacrifice, austerity and alms-giving are each of three kinds — Sattwa, Rajas, and Tamas (17 : 7).

When men offer sacrifice in accordance with scriptural instructions, and do not desire any advantage for themselves, they are inspired by 'Sattwa'. Their hearts are set upon the sacrifice for its own sake. An inner sense of duty impels them to discharge their duties (17 : 11, 17 : 20, 23 : 26).

The performance of sacrifice for outward show or in the hope of reward is inspired by 'Rajas' (17 : 12, 21,24, 27).

Austerity which is practised out of selfish pride or in indifference to the interest of others, or to harm the reputation of another person in Tamas (17 : 13, 19, 22; 18 : 25, 28).

Respectful homage to Gods, Brāhmaṇas, revered elders, and wise men, purity, uprightness, chastity and harmlessness constitute the austerity of the body. Words that cause no disturbance to others are true and beneficial, and recitation of sacred texts constitute the austerity of speech. Serenity of mind, kindliness, silence, self control, and purification of self constitute the austerity of the mind.

O Arjuna! work done without sincerity and devotion is of no use either in this or the next world (17 : 28).

This small chapter of the Gītā furnishes a touch-stone for human actions and intentions.

CHAPTER XVIII

In this last chapter, the Gītā exposes the outward show of the Sanyāsa observance of rituals :

> The renouncing of acts of desire,
> Sages call renunciation.
> The abandonment of all action-fruits,
> The wise call abandonment. (2 : 18)

Wherever reference is made in the Gītā to renunciation and abandonment, it means that the devotee, while performing his duty, should not pay heed to the result, be that pleasure or pain, honour or dishonour. His mind should remain entirely unaffected by them.

This does not mean that he should attend to his duty or work without thinking of results. As stated in the preceding chapters, any work done without thinking is very evilsome, or 'tamas'. On the other hand, whatever work is done, it should be free from self-interest, and it should be done for the welfare of others. This is renunciation or 'sanyāsa' or 'tyāga'. (3 :25).

Acts of sacrifice, alms-giving and austerity lead to the purity of mind. But even such a kind of work should be done as a duty discharged for its own sake and without any regard for its results (18 : 5, 6).

This is real renunciation and abandonment or non-attachment (18 : 9, 11).

To abandon duty under the stress of the ego or to neglect it for fear of physical pain is of course evilsome (18 : 7-8)

Knowledge is of three kinds. To know and to see one God, the Immortal and the Undefinable, in all creatures, despite their varieties, is 'Sāttwik'. To see 'Ātma' differently in different objects is 'Rajas'. To pursue a thing blindly under a delusion, and in utter disregard of reality, is 'Tamas' (18 : 20-22).

To regard all faiths and castes as one and the same is Sāttwik. To regard them as different from one another is 'Rajas'. To consider one's own faith and caste as the right and those of others as the wrong is 'Tamas'.

Happiness also is of three kinds. The happiness which is bitter in the beginning and sweet in the long run, bringing contentment to both mind and soul, is Sāttwik, is good. The senses which are sweet in the beginning and bitter in the end partake of 'Rajas', passion. But the pleasure which excites the body from beginning to end, and finally throws one into stupor or sloth is 'Tamas', darkness (18 : 37, 38, 39).

In the same way, Kartā, Karma, Buddhi, and Dhairya are each of three kinds.

While admitting that all faiths preach the practice of virtue and lay emphasis on the need to see one and the same Ātma in different objects, the Gītā recognises different ways of life for different men. It admits only one difference, and that is the difference in individual temperament or tendencies. The Gītā does not recognise differences of birth or caste or country or community, but is prepared to classify mankind under the different professional occupations in which different men engage themselves in accordance with their inherent aptitudes or talents (18 : 41-44).

In this, there is no question of great or small, of low or of high birth or caste, because men can attain perfection in their respective lines, provided they do so for the sake of Paraméśwara who has created them and who dwells in all (18 : 45-46).

Every one's assigned duties constitute his own faith and he should not trespass on another's faith.

While indicating how man can know Paraméśwara, the Gītā states once again :

When man's mind and heart are freed from illusions, when he has mastered his self, when no desire pulsates in his heart, when he has subdued his senses and abandoned all pleasures emanating therefrom without regret or aversion, when he seeks solitude, and eats but little and curbs his speech, and meditates on his soul and has totally thrown off vanity, pride, lust, anger, and all his possessions and his sense of ego, and is tranquil of heart, it is then that he puts on a divine visage. It is then that his mind remains unperturbed by anything, and his heart is filled with happiness, and he regards all creatures with an equal eye. It is in this way that he understands God properly and with a mind made serene, he attains union with Him (18 : 49-55)

Emphasis is laid repeatedly on doing a thing for the sake of Īśwara alone (18 : 57).

At the end of the Gītā, the greatest of all secrets is revealed in the following words:

Further, the highest secrect of all
My supreme message, hear,
Because thou art greatly loved of Me.
Therefore I shall tell thee what is good for thee.
Be Me-minded; devoted to Me;
Worshipping Me, revere Me;
And to Me alone shalt thou go; truly to thee
I promise it - (because) thou art dear to Me.
Abandoning all (other) duties
Go to Me as thy sole refuge;
From all evils I thee
Shall rescue: be not grieved! (18 : 64, 65, 66).

THE ESSENCE OF THE GĪTĀ

As pointed out in the very beginning of the volume, we have endeavoured to present only the Dhārmic aspect of the Gītā which in our opinion is of universal value to people of every age and country. In our rendering of the original, we have taken care to see that instead of translating the matter, stanza by stanza, line by line, the essence of the entire thought-content under each chapter is clearly presented to the mind of the reader. The Gītā, no doubt, discusses in its own peculiar fashion what relation subsists between soul and God or Paramēśwara, how He is both Transcendent and Immanent, what is matter and what is soul, how the universe came into existence, and so forth, and also how the Gītā in spite of its leanings towards advaitic view of life, upholds in the interests of righteous or Dhārmic living, the belief in One Supreme Īshwara, and why it does not regard compelling to entertain any belief in advaitism or similar stand-points.

The religion of the Gītā is a practical religion laying down a programme of action and is not a code of mere beliefs.

We now propose to sum up the contents of the teaching of the Gītā, in but a few paragraphs.

In the days of the Gītā, society was composed of numerous castes and families formed on the basis of birth. From time immemorial, each caste and each family had come to observe a particular code of Dharma consisting of customs, rites and rituals peculiar to each (1 : 40, 44). The observance of caste or family Dharma was considered so essential to life that any negligence on the part of the caste or family concerned was believed to result in the consignment to hell of every member of that caste or family, male and female, both living and the already dead (1 : 42). The dead were offered articles of food by their progeny (1 : 42). Naturally therefore any inter-mixture of castes or families was dreaded, and it was regarded as a heinecus sin to kill or exterminate a member of one's own family, however cruel or undesirable he might be (1 : 36, 45). The Gītā, on the other hand, regards the observance of rites and rituals as a sign of weakness of heart and unworthy of man (2 : 2-10). The people of the times believed in the three Vēdas—Ṛg, Yajur and Sāma. It was from these Vēdas that they had learnt the ways of performing Yajña, Havan, Japam, Tapas etc. People worshipped many demi-gods and goddesses. To these deities, a variety of animal sacriffces were offered by way of appeasement. The deities were bedecked with costly jewels, and their aid was invoked in the fulfilment of a variety of desires, both spiritual and sensuous. On occasions of Yajña, wine or Sōma was used (2 : 42, 44, 53).

The Gītā called upon the people of the time to rise superior to these rites and rituals. It regarded them as mere superstition, and the people who performed them as an unthinking lot (2 : 42-44). The people were enmeshed in the Karma Kāṇḍa of the Vēdas and needed to extricate themselves from its clutches. For a thoughtful man, the Vēdas were as useless as the water of a well situated in the midst of a vast expanse of pure water (2 : 45-46). The teaching of the Vēdas undermines the mind of man (2 : 53). He who truly practises the Karma Yōga or fulfils his duties conscientiously does not need the Vēdas (6 : 44). One cannot enter into the presence of Īśwara by following the Vēdas or performing Yajña, Japam or Tapas (11 : 48, 52).

The Gītā describes clearly what true Yagña is or Tapas or the rest. In the fourth chapter, while referring to the various forms of Yajña performed in those days, the Gītā points out that the true Yajña lies in discarding one's selfishness

(4 : 23), in entertaining no ill-will towards any body, in doing good to others and in worshipping Īśwara for the sake of Īśwara only (4 : 22-24). This is Yajña, it states : and the greatest Yajña is that which it calls Jñāna Yajña by which man sees the entire world in his own being, and sees every thing in the being of Īśwara (4 : 35). There is nothing more purifying than this Yajña or Gnosis (4 : 38). Similarly, the Gītā regards the state of Brahmacharya (control of desires) and Ahiṁsa (dissuading oneself from harming others) as the tapas of the body, the speaking of a word that does not hurt any one and which promotes the good of others as the tapas of the tongue, and the control of desires, the purification of the heart. and the cultivation of peace of mind as the tapas of the mind (17 : 14-16).

The Gītā regards the pleasures of the senses and the temptations of Heaven as obstacles to spiritual progress and advises man not to be enticed by them. It displays a special attitude towards the traditional religious rites and rituals. Since ignorant folk, in the pursuit of these rituals, very often do good deeds, it is part of wisdom not to disturb their belief in rituals, lest they should turn away from doing good deeds (3 : 26-29).

The Gītā holds likewise a special attitude towards the worship of demi-gods or forces of nature on the one hand, and of the worship of One Supreme God or Īśwara on the other. In respect of Īśwara, the Gīta holds that He has no beginning and no end ; it permeates all phenomenal objects and yet is different from them ; it dwells in the hearts of all, and yet is beyond the reach of thought; neither the human mind can comprhend it, nor the human tongue describe Him fully. It is difficult for the human intellect to catch the reality of such a transcendent Being (12 : 3-5). So, man may worship Him in some attribute or other of that Being. Each attribute is personified in a deity or demi-god or a spiritual man. In this way, all the demigods are, in their several forms, regarded as the several attributes or aspects of the Divinity in Īśwara. The worship of any one of these demi-gods, the Gītā regards, is in a way the worship of Īśwara Himself.

Islam regards the worship of anything besides the trancendent Being of God as wrong and rigidly discountenances it. But the view advanced of the Gītā just above is entertained in some Sūfi works. In the 17th century of Christian era, there lived in Allahabad a Sūfi by name Shaik Muhibbullah. In his published correspondence in Persian with Dārā Shikōḥ in which Shaik Muhibbullah, while explaining the meaning of the credal formula, Lā Illāha Illallāh (Tnere is none worthy of worship except God), he states: "All the deities worshipped in the world are all Allāh". The famous work on Sūfism "Gulshani-Rāz" takes exactly the same view. In the opinion of the Sūfis of this category who believe in Advaitism or wahadut-al Wajūd or the Unity of Being, God is one only, that there is none like unto Him, and that the deities or objects of devotion are the forms of one and the same Allāh and that therefore the worship of them, in a way, is the worship of Allāh Himself.* The thought of these Sūfis is more or less the same as that held by the Gītā. The Gītā holds the view that one who sincerely offers his devotion, in his own way, is in that same way acceptable to God (4 : 11).

In whatsoever way any come to Me,
In that same way I grant them favour.
My path follow
Men altogether, son of Pṛtha. (4 : 11)

While the Gītā regards the worship of the different demigods as irregular (9 : 23), that which is offered to the demi-gods goes to the demi-gods, it says, and that which is offered to Īśwara goes to Īśwara (9 : 25). The Gītā therefore repeatedly asserts that one should give up the worship of demi-gods and offer exclusive devotion to Īśwara alone (9 : 27,34), and giving

* The essential Sufii view is not exactly the same as is attributed in the text to Shaik Muhibullah Shah or to the author of Gulshan-i-Rāz, Mahmūd Shabistarī. Those who believe in "Wahadut-al-'Wajūd' or 'Unity of Being' or 'Unity of Existence' distinguish between 'Existence (Wajūd) and Existent (Mawjūd)' and between the 'Self-Existence' of God (Wajūd-bil-Zāt) and the 'Derived Existence' of the phenomenal object (Wajūd-bil-Arḍ)' and indeed regard God alone as the Reality of Being, and the phenomenal object as but its shadow or reflection, nay, illusion; so much so, that their conception of devotion to God stands on all fours with that presented by the Qur'ān, expressly marking out devotion to anything beside God, the Absolute, as 'Shirk'.—Ed.

up all Dharmas, one should seek refuge only in Īśwara, for, He alone can protect one from sins (18 : 66).

So, the Gītā and the Qur'ān enjoin the worship of none except the Only One God.

The Gītā regards the order of castes — Brāhmaṇa, Kṣatriya, Vysya, Śūdra — as based not on birth but on aptitudes and does not regard any one of them as superior to any other in his intrinsic worth. He who can keep his desires under control, whose heart is restful and who engages himself in activities pertinent to his aptitudes; it is he alone who should be called a Brāhmaṇa. The man who displays courage and who has talent for administration, he should be called a Kṣatriya; the agriculturist and the trader should be called Vysya; and the man engaged in handicrafts Śūdra (18 : 42-44). The Gītā clearly points out that castes should not be based on birth, family, or any special religious creed. The four types of people will be found in every society throughout the world. If the words of the Gītā are to be believed, all those Brāhmaṇas and Kṣatriyas employed in India, either in the government service or in the field of labour, should be regarded as Śūdras, the Muslim Borahs of Bombay as Vysyas, and thousands of non-Hindus like Rev. C. F. Andrews and Mawlana Abul Kalam Azad as Brāhmaṇas.

From the philosophic standpoint, two schools of thought prevailed in the days of the Gītā. One was of those who believed in the karma kāṇda of Vēdas and the rites and rituals prescribed by them and who considered that salvation lay only in observing them. On the other hand, there was the school of thought who believed in the Sāṅkhya system of life which enjoined the way of sanyāsa and tyāga. The Gītā while declaring itself against the outward forms of observances under the two systems, tried to reconcile one with the other (5 : 4-5). The Gītā says that he who does not touch fire or who is obsessed with only the outward forms of ceremonials is not a true sanyāsi. Nor does it call one a karma yōgi who is a slave to passions and desires or attaches undue importance to ceremonials. He who has discarded selfish desires from his mind and rises superior to the senses of otherness, entertains no ill-feeling towards anyone, and who has discharged his obligations to others is truly a sanyāsi and a true yōgi (5 : 3; 6 : 1).

The right way of life or Dharma which the Gītā enjoins on one and all, and on which it lays repeated emphasis is this : "He alone is Dharmātma who subdues his senses by keeping control over them (12 : 4), who rises superior to the sense of otherness and who unmindful of his own happiness, and insensitive to the prospects of gain or loss (2 : 38), aims at the welfare of everyone (3 : 25), who without entertaining any ill-will against any one (11 : 55), engages himself in the welfare of others (5 : 25; 12 : 14) and who discharges his duty for its own sake (18 : 9). The Gītā says that there are three gates to Hell—desire, wrath and greed (16 : 21). This is the sum and substance of the teaching of the Gītā. To follow it, says the Gītā, is to observe true devotion to Īśwara (12 : 13-20). It says : he is the most dear to Īśwara who is not feared by any one in the world and who fears none (12 : 15). On the other hand, the life of one who, in self-interest and out of egoism, performs the arduous practices of tapas, his life is satanic, and Īśwara is not pleased with such a man (16 : 5-6). On the other hand, he who, controlling his self, does his duty to others, and actively cares for them, attains true Knowledge or gnosis. The true gnosist is to regard others even as one's own self (5 : 7; 6 : 32), and to see the entire world in one's self (6 : 29), and to see the entire world in Īśwara and Īśwara Himself in everything (6 : 30-31). It is by 'Ātmasīnam' and service to others that man can purify his soul and enter upon the road to perfection, and it is by feeling the presence of Paramātma in his own self and in the entire phenomenal world, that he can behold the countenance of Īśwara who is the jyōti of jyōtis or light of lights, (3 : 17) and who dwells in the heart of everyone (15 : 15), and thus attain salvation (3 : 19; 5 : 16; 17 : 30). This is the ESSENCE of the message of the Gītā.

THE QU'RĀN

The soul of Muhammad, the Prophet of Islam, was among the most searching souls of the world. It was after years of meditation, seclusion, fasts and vigils, spent in reflecting over the degarded condition of the Arabs of his time, that God showed to him the way of salvation of the people of his own country and of the world at large. Before he could deliver his message, he had already reached his 40 years. He was 63 when he passed away. Within the period of 23 years, whenever he was confronted with any spiritual struggle, and could not find a way out, he usually sought the light of God through tearful prayers. On such occasions, his body used to shiver. At times, he wrapped himself in a blanket and lay down, tears and perspiration often soaking his blanket. At times, for days together, he used to lie down in this way without touching a morsel of food or a drop of water. Whenever he rose from this state and gave utterance to anything, he designated the utterance as the word of God. Utterances of this nature which were uttered forth from time to time during these 23 years are collected together under the name of the Qurā'n.

The term 'Qurā'n' is derived from Vira which means to proclaim or announce. The Sanskrit 'krid', the English 'cry', and the Arabic 'qirah' come from the same root. The literary meaning of the Qur'ān is that which is announced or read out. The traditional meaning of it is "The Book of Religion".

Before the advent of Islam, the Jews called their scripture 'Qarah'. The Hebrew language of the Jews, and the Arabic of the Arabs are closely allied together. The Qur'ān and Qarah bear the same meaning. In fact the Qur'ān calls each of the scriptures delivered before it as Qur'ān (Q. 15 : 18, 91).

The sayings of the Prophet and the first hand accounts of his work are called Hadith. These are not regarded as inspired or revealed.

The passages of the Qur'ān as delivered from time to time were under the direction of the Prophet recorded on palm leaves, pieces of skin, or slabs or planks. At times, these were taken up by his followers for reading out; but a good many of them were used to be committed to memory. These several pieces of record were kept in a box with no effort at arrangement. The collection gradually gathered volume. Certain portions of these were, during the time of the Prophet, pieced together to form chapters or parts.

It is stated in the Qur'ān: "Whatever verse we cancel, or cause to forget, we bring a better or its like. Knowest thou not that God hath power over all things." (Q. 2 : 106). In another place, the Qur'ān states: "We change one Āyat (sign or verse) for another, and God knoweth best what He revealeth (Q. 16 : 101).

In this way, it is stated on the authority of the work "The Wisdom of the Qur'ān" by Muhammad Muktar Pasha (Introduction—page 45) that 60 Āyat were cancelled during the life time of the Prophet and a few others which fell into disuse after him also came to be regarded as cancelled.*

---

*The Arabic word Āyat (plural Āyāt) posseses a variety of connotations. (Vide Arabic English Lexicon compiled by E W- Lane— Book I, Part I), In the context of the passages quoted from the Qur'ān, It means a ve se or a portion of any revealed scripture denoting an ordinance of God. The reference is to the ordinances, not of the Qur'ān itself, as is made out in the text, but to ordinarces revealed to previous prophets from time to time. Mawlāna Abul Kalām Azād in his commentary of the Qur'ān, entitled *Tarjimān-al-Qur'ān* writes under the verse (Q. 2 : 106) as follows:

"One ordinance followed another, either in the state of 'Naskh' or 'Nisyān'. 'Naskh' means an ordinance fallen into disuse and replaced by another. 'Nisyān' means to forget. So it happened under certain situations. The previous ordinance was in one form or another stlll in existence, but the atomosphere for it or the conditions of its operation had changed or the urge to follow it was lacking. In such a situation, the promulgation of a new ordinance became necessary. At times, it so happened that through the exigencies of time, the old ordinance was forgotten. Necessarily therefore, it had to be revived. The way of God is

The word 'Āyat' bears the same meaning as 'Richa' in the Vēdas.

Khalif Abū Bakr, the first Khalif of the Prophet, collected all the passages of the Qur'ān available at the Prophet's house or preserved by different personages, and divided them into 14 parts. The collection was handed to the Prophet's widow Ḥafsa for safe keeping. Copies of some of the passages were already with a number of people. Besides a good many passages had been committed to memory and ultimately reduced to writing. The result was that within 15 years of the death of the Prophet various collections under the name of the Qur'ān came to be in use in the different parts of the Arab State, one varying with another in certain respects. It was in the time of the Third Khalif, Uthmān, that the need was felt to issue an authorised version of the Qur'ān. The copy that had been preserved with the Prophet's widow Ḥafsa was obtained from her by the Khalif and declared to be the authentic version. Copies of this were made out and distributed in all the centres of Muslim population, enjoining that from that time onward this was the version that was to be regarded as the version used by the Prophet. The copies of the other versions were collected and burnt. The authorised version issued by Khalif Uthman is thus the only version that has been in use ever since throughout the Muslim world.

Notwithstanding the care thus observed, there still exist seven variations of the Qur'ān; but the variation is not in the text: it is only in the numbering of verses. For instance, in one variation, one verse stands divided into two verses. Thus, one version of the Qur'ān marks 6000 verses, two versions show 6214, the fourth 6219, the fifth 6236, the sixth 6246, and the last 6225. But the text is one and the same in all.

There is one stupendous difficulty which one feels in the reading of the Qur'ān. The passages in the different

---

that every new teaching is either superior to the earlier teaching (whether forgotten or fallen into disuse) or similar to it. It is never lower in type than the earlier teaching; for the movement in life is always forward or evolutionary and not retrogressive.

The consensus of opinion among the 'Ulamā' has been that no Āyat of the Qurā'n was ever abrogated.

—Translator.

parts of it are not pieced-together in the order in which they were delivered. In other words, they are not arranged chronologically. A later sura or chapter comes in the early parts and an early sura in the closing parts, and even in a single sura the later verses come first and the earlier verses next to them. It is therefore not possible to say which verse was delivered when and in what circumstances or in response to what situation. A large majority of the verses no doubt have been assigned by consensus of opinion to particular times in the life of the Prophet. Still, a good deal of difference exists among scholars in respect of the rest. This is the difficulty which faces a casual reader of the Qur'ān. Those who know Arabic may catch the essence of the Qur'ān as a whole; but the case of those who recite the Qur'ānic passages merely for ritual purposes without knowing their meaning is different. Still, those who care to understand the contents of the Qur'ān may easily piece together verses falling under particular themes and gather a comprehensive view of each subject presented therein.

THE LANGUAGE OF THE QUR'ĀN

The opinion of Arab and non-Arab scholars is that the style of the Qur'ān is exalted, highly melodious and sweet. It is a sort of poetic prose or free verse. The most scholarly of its English translators, George Sale says:

> "The style of the Koran is generally beautiful and fluent. It is concise and often obscure, adorned with bold figures after the eastern taste, enlivened with florid and sententious expressions, and in many places, especially where the majesty and attributes of God are described, sublime and magnificent."
>
> (The Koran: Translation into English by George sale. A Priliminary Discourse. P. 48).

The manners of reciting the Qur'ān are as diverse as the manners of reciting the Vēdas.

PRE-ISLAMIC ARABS:

We have pieced together below under separate heads various verses of the Qur'ān. The idea is to facilitate an easy grasp of the contents of the Qur'ān. There are extensive passages in the Qur'ān which speak of communities and societies who had come to grief for having deviated from the path of Dharma or righteousness. There are also in the Qur'ān various injunctions or commandments issued from time to time on particular occasions in the course of the Prophetic mission.

To understand the Qur'ānic message, it may be necessary to get at least a fleeting view of the state of affairs among the Arabs when the Qur'ān came to be delivered among them.

At the time of the prophet the Arabs were divided into tribes, big and small. These tribes were in perennial warfare with each other. Every tribe came to regard itself as independent of every other. Each tribe had its tribal deity, whom they worshipped. The deities were carved in stone and wood or in moulded unlevened flour. The deities were given shapes of men or women or animals or trees, and some were merely shapeless lumps.

A good many of the tribes worshipped a multitude of these deities, both male and female. The idea of a supreme God was nearly absent among them. Nor had they any common view of righteous living. One was against another. There was nothing in their several lives which could bind them together in a single chain of fraternal relations. The result was that the major parts of the Arab land had come under the sway of foreign governments. The north was under the grip of the Christian Roman Imeprial rule; the east was held by the Khosores of Iran, and the south and west by the Christian Ethiopia. More than half of the Arab land was thus under the foreign yoke.

The life of the people had grown so vicious that deaths due to drunkenness were common. Gambling went apace so freely with drink that numerous Arabs having lost all their material resources, went to the length of staking even their personal liberty and become slaves of winners.

The slaves were treated in those days as mere chattel. Even like cattle, they were sold or purchased freely in the market. Indeed, children were snatched away from the laps of their mothers and sold in the open market. The mother went as purchased commodity to one and the child to another. No punishment was meted out to anyone who destroyed a slave. Fornication with a female slave was freely allowed. At times, the slave owners made money by forcing their female slaves to fetch them money by prostitution. The Arabs had grown so depraved that they openly prided themselves on their depravity.

The women folk were, in general, treated shabbily. They enjoyed no personal rights. A man could marry as many wives as he liked and divorce them whenever he liked. A practice also was in vogue to have several common husbands for a single woman. Nights and days of the week were distributed serially among the husbands. The father of the family dying, the eldest son became the owner of his wives except his own mother or his foster mother, and there was no other relationship which was held sacred. The Arab regarded it a personal affront to own a son-in-law. Sometimes, a female child was buried alive as soon as it was born. Even children of the age of five or six were buried to avoid the disgrace of having sons-in-law on their account.

Usury was rampant in the Arab land.

Along with these vices, the Arab life had certain redeeming features. It was marked by personal bravery, hospitality and respect for promises made. But these redeeming features were overshadowed by their life in other directions. The condition of the Arabs at the time when the Prophet was born was indeed deplorable. We have to keep this fact in view when we study the Qur'ān.

THE INFLUENCE OF THE QUR'ĀN:

The Qur'ān rooted out from the Arab life a good many of their poisonous vices such as drunkenness, gambling, usury, and the burying alive of female children. It taught those who used to worship thousands of demi-gods to worship but one Supreme God of all creation. It welded together hundreds of warring tribes into a single Arab nation, and raised high their standard of conduct and morality. It inspired in them the love of knowledge. It freed the different parts of the Arab land from foreign yoke and converted it into a single Arab State. All this was achieved in the brief span of but 23 years.

Within a century of the death of the Prophet, the new faith of the Arabs spread to the Chinese Wall, on the one hand, and the Atlantic Ocean, on the other, covering the whole of West Asia, the whole of North Africa, and one half of Europe, and energized the Arabs to lead the nations of the world in the field of art, science and philosophy.

Today, more than three hundred million souls may easily be counted among the followers of the Qurā'n, and there is not a single country in the world today where there are not people who seek the way of good life from this Book.

A well-known European Scholar, Arthur Glyn Leonard, sums up the achievements of the Qurā'n during the last 1300 years and over in the following words:

> "If a book is to be guaged by its nett results, by the effect it has produced on all that is deepest and best in human nature, then, the Qur'ān must necessarily take a high rank as one of the world's Greatest Works." *

A few years ago a leading monthly magazine of Europe sent round a circular to the leading professors of the Universities of the West requesting them to furnish it a list of the greatest books of the world. Hundreds of replies were received in response to the request. The first prize was given to the *Iliad* of Homer written a thousand years before Christ. The second place was given to the Qur'ān. The verdict, be it remembered, is the verdict of a body of scholars everyone of whom was a European and most of whom had formed their opinion not on the basis of having read the original in Arabic but from the impression formed of it through mere translation of it in the European languages.

---

* *Islam* by Major Arthur Glyn Leonard, Pp. 105 - 106.

THE QUR'ĀN AND ITS TEACHING

The first chapter of the Qur'ān is styled Al-Fātiha. It is called by the Qur'ān itself (Q 15 : 87) as the "Grand Qur'ān". Even as the entire book is called the Qur'ān, every part of it also is called the Qur'ān, and Al-Fātiha occupies a pre-eminent position therein, and is consequently styled the Grand Qur'ān. The Prophet used to refer to it as the "Mother of the Qur'ān" (Bukhari). It is generally regarded as the 'Essence' of the Qur'ān, and is consequently repeated frequently in Muslim worship and prayers. "Al-Fātiha" means "the opening". It runs as follows :

In the name of Allāh, the Beneficent, the Merciful!
Praise be to God, Lord of all the worlds!
The Beneficent, the Merciful!
King on the day of requital!
Thee alone do we worship, and Thee alone do we ask
for help.
Show us the straight path,
The path of those to whom thou hast been gracious;
Not of those with whom thou are not pleased,
Nor of those who have gone astray, Amen!

THE BASIC DOCTRINES OF ISLAM

" Say : He, God is one :
God is He on whom all depend.
He begetteth not ; and He is not begotten ;
And there is none like unto Him. (Q. 112 : 1-4)

No doubt is there about this Book: It is a guidance to the God-fearing.

Who believe in the unseen, who observe prayer, and out of what we have bestowed on them, expend for God,

And who believe in what hath been sent down to thee, and in what hath been sent down before thee, and full faith have they in the life to come.

These are guided by their Lord; and with these it shall be well. (Q. 2 : 2-5)

PRAISE OF GOD

Has thou not seen how all in the Heavens and in the Earth utter the praise of God? — the very birds as they spread their wings? Every creature knoweth its prayer and its praise, and God knoweth what they do.

God's the Kingdom of the Heavens and of the Earth: and unto God the final return!

Hast thou not seen that God driveth clouds lightly forward, then gathereth them together, then pileth them in masses? And then thou seest the rain forthcoming from their midst; and He causeth clouds like mountains charged with hail, to descend from the heaven, and He maketh it to fall on whom He will, and from whom He will, He turneth it aside — The brightness of His lightning all but taketh away the sight!

God causeth the day and the night to take their turn. Verily in this is teaching for men of insight. And God hath created every animal of water. Some go upon the belly; some go upon two feet; some go upon four feet. God hath created what he pleased. Aye, God hath power over all things. (Q. 24 : 41-45)

Sole maker of the Heavens and the Earth! He hath created everything, and He knoweth everything. This is God your Lord. There is no God but He, the creator of all things: therefore worship Him alone, and he watcheth over all things.

No vision taketh in Him, but He taketh in all vision: and He is the Subtile, the All- informed. (Q. 6 : 102-103)

God! There is no God but he; the Living, the Eternal. Nor slumber seizeth him; nor sleep. His whatsoever is in the

Heavens and whatsoever is in the Earth! Who is He that can intercede with Him but by His own permission? He knoweth what hath been before them and what shall be after them: yet nought of His knowledge shall they grasp, save what He willeth. His Throne reacheth over the Heavens and the Earth, and the upholding of both burdeneth Him not; and He is the High, the Great!

(Q. 2:256)

And when my servants ask thee concerning me, then will I be nigh unto them. I will answer the cry of him that crieth, when he crieth unto me; but let them hearken unto Me, and believe in Me, that they may proceed aright. (Q. 2 : 182)

We created man: and we know what his soul whispereth to him, and we are close to him than his jugular vein.

(Q. 50:15)

And whatever suffering ye suffer, it is what your hands have wrought: and yet He forgiveth many things.

(Q. 41 : 29)

Say: O my servants who have transgressed against their own souls, despair not of God's mercy, for all sins doth God forgive. Gracious, Merciful is He. (Q. 39 : 54)

God is the most merciful of those who show mercy.

(Q. 12:92)

To those who have done evil in ignorance, then afterwards have repented and amended, verily thy Lord is in the end right, gracious, merciful. (Q. 16:120)

Yet he who doth evil, or wrongeth his own soul and then seeketh pardon of God, will find God Forgiving, Merciful.

And whoever committeth a crime, committeth it to his own hurt. And God is knowing, Wise!

And whoever committeth an involuntary fault or a crime, and then layeth it on the innocent, shall surely bear the guilt of calumny and of a manifest crime.

(Q. 4 : 110-112)

But whoever shall turn him to God after this his wickedness, and amend, God truly will be turned to him: for God is Forgiving, Merciful. (Q. 5 : 43)

Surely, however, will I forgive him who turneth to God and believeth, and worketh righteousness, and then yieldeth to guidance. (Q. 20 : 84)

To hasten evil rather than good will they challenge thee: but, before their time have been like examples. Full, truly of mercy is thy Lord unto men, despite their sins; but verily thy Lord is strict in punishment. (Q. 13:7)

And is He the Indulgent, the Loving. (Q. 85:14)

God is Truth (Q. 22:62)

God is the LIGHT of the Heavens and of the earth. His Light is like a niche in which is a lamp—the lamp encased in glass—the glass, as it were, a glistening star. From a blessed tree is it lighted, the olive neither of the East nor of the West, whose oil would well nigh shine out, even though fire touched it not! It is light upon light.

God guideth whom He will to His light, and God setteth forth parables to men, for God knoweth all things. (Q. 24:35)

Wherever ye turn, ye will find the countenance of God. (Q. 2:115)

If all the trees that are upon the earth were to become pens, and if God should after that swell the sea into seven seas of ink, His words would not be exhausted: for God is Mighty, Wise. (Q. 31:26)

And think within thine own self on God, with lowliness, and with fear and without loud spoken words, at even and at morn; and be not one of the heedless. (Q. 7:204)

And observe prayer at early morning, at the close of the day, and at the approach of night; for the good deeds drive away the evil deeds. This is a warning for those who reflect: And persevere steadfastly, for verily God will not suffer the reward of the righteous to perish. (Q. 11:116-117)

MANKIND BUT ONE COMMUNITY

Mankind were but one community only: then they fell to variance. (Q. 10:20)

Of truth, this your religion (or community) is the one Religion (or community) and I am your Lord; therefore serve Me:

But they have rent asunder this as their great concern among themselves into sects. All of them shall return to us. (Q. 21:92-93)

No kind of beast is there on earth nor fowl that flieth with its wings, but is a folk like you: nothing have we passed over in the Book; then unto their Lord shall they be gathered". (Q. 6 : 38)

MESSAGE OF DIVINE UNITY DELIVERED TO ALL

Verily, they, who belive (in that which is revealed to thee, Muhammad) and they who are Jews, and Christians, and Sabeites — whoever of these believeth in God and the last day, and doeth that which is right, surely, they shall have their reward with their Lord: fear shall not come upon them, neither shall they grieve. (Q. 2 : 59)

Verily, they who believe, and the Jews, and the Sabeites, and the Christians — whoever of them believeth in God and in the last day, and doeth what is right; on them shall come no fear, neither shall they grieve. (Q. 5 : 69)

And they say, "None but Jews or Christians shall enter Paradise: This is their wish, Say, Give your proofs if ye speak the truth:

But they who set their face with resignation God-ward, and do what is right, — their reward is with their Lord: no fear shall come on them, neither shall they grieve." (Q. 2: 105-106)

"Apostles truly have we already sent before thee, and wives and offspring have we given them. Yet no apostle had come with miracles unless by the leave of God. For everything there is a time prescribed.

What He pleaseth will God efface or establish (what He will); with Him is the source of revelation." (Q. 13: 38-39)

"To every pophecy is its set time, and bye-and-bye ye shall know it." (Q. 6: 66)

"O children of Adam! there shall come to you Apostles from among yourselves, rehearsing my signs to you; and whoso shall fear God and do good works, no fear shall come on them, neither shall they grieve," (Q. 7 : 33)

"And every people hath had its apostle." (Q. 10: 48)

"And every people hath had its guide." (Q. 13 : 8)

"Verily we have sent thee with thee truth; a bearer of good tiding and a warner; nor hath there been a people unvisited by its warner;" (Q. 35: 32)

"And already have we sent apostles, before thee, among the ancient peoples". (Q. 15 : 10)

"We sent Apostles to nations before thee, but Satan made their deeds fair-seeming unto them, and this day is he their liege; and a woeful punishment doth await them." (Q. 16 : 65)

"And we have never sent a messenger save with the speech of his own people, that he might make (the message) clear for them." (Q. 14 : 4)

"Say ye: We believe in God, and that which hath been sent down to us, and that which hath been sent down to Abraham and Ismael and Isaac and Jacob and the tribes: and that which hath been given to Moses and to Jesus, and that which was given to the prophets from their Lord. No difference do we make between any of them: and to God are we resigned." (Q. 2 : 130)

"The apostle believeth in that which hath been sent down from his Lord, as do the faithful also. Each one believeth in God, and His Angels, and His books, and His Apostles: we make no distinction between any of His Apostles. And they say, "We have heard and we obey. Thy mercy, Lord! for unto thee must we return." (Q. 2 : 285)

"Recite that which hath been inspired in thee and discharge the duty of prayer: for prayer restraineth from lewdness and inequity. And the gravest duty is the remembrance of God and God knoweth what ye do. Argue not, unless in kindly sort, with the people of the Book; save with such of them as have dealt wrongfully with you: And say ye, "We believe in what hath been sent down to us and hath been sent down to you. Our God and your God is one, and to him do we surrender" (Muslims)* (Q. 29 : 44-45)

* The two terms 'Muslim' and 'Islam' have been used in numerous places in the Qur'ān. 'Islam' is derived from 'Salama' which means 'to bow one's head or' to submit one's wish to another's wish'. 'Islam' thus means complete surrender to the Will of God', and 'Muslim' or 'Musalman' means 'one who has completely surrendered himself to God'. It is in this sense that the Qur'ān in several places calls the religions delivered before the Prophet Muhammad as 'Islam' and those who believe in them as 'Muslims'.

Further, the word 'Islam' denotes peace or shanti. It is in this sense that the Qur'ān uses the terms in verse (10 : 25), but the essential sense is as explained above, viz., to submit to the Will of God in the manner suggested by the Qur'ān.

O ye apostles! eat of things that are good: and do that which is right: of your doings I am cognizant.

And truly this your religion is the one religion: and I am your Lord: therefore fear me.

But men have rent their concern, one among another into sects; every party rejoicing in that which is their own;

Wherefore leave them till a certain time, in their depths of error. (Q. 23:53-55)

"Of a truth they who believe not on God and His Apostles, and seek to separate God from his Apostles, and say, " Some we believe, and some we believe not " and desire to take a middle way;

These! they are veritable infidels! and for the infidels have we prepared a shameful punishment." (Q. 4:149-150)

"Verily whe have revealed to thee as we revealed to Noah and the Prophets after him, and as we revealed to Abraham, and Ismael, and Issac, and Jacob, and the tribes, and Jesus, and Job, and Jonah, and Aaron, and Solomon; and to David gave we Psalms.

Of some apostles we have told thee before: of other apostles we have not told thee. (Q. 4:161-162)

"Already have we sent apostles to nations that were before thee." (Q. 6:43)

"We send not our messengers but as heralds of good news and warners; and whoso shall believe and amend, on them shall come no fear, neither shall they grieve. (Q. 6:48)

"As to those who split up their religion and become sects' have thou nothing to do with them: their affair is with God only. Hereafter shall he tell them what they have done." (Q. 6:160)

"For he it is who by God's leave hath caused the Koran to descend on thy heart, the confirmation of previous revelation, and guidance, and good tidings to the faithful." (Q. 2:91)

And when there came to them an apostle from God, affirming the previous revelations made to them, some of those to whom the Scriptures were given threw the Book of God behind their backs as if they knew it not. (Q. 2:95)

Verily, we have sent Thee with the Truth; a bearer of good tidings and a warner; nor hath there been a people unvisited by its warner. (Q. 35:22)

Nay, He (Prophet Muhammad) cometh with truth, and confirmeth the sent ones, of old previous scriptures. (Q. 37 : 37)

Nothing hath been said to thee which hath not been said of old to apostles before thee. (Q. 41 : 43)

But before the Koran was the Book of Moses, a rule and a mercy, and this Book confirmeth it (the Pentateuch)—in the Arabic tongue—that those who are guilty of wrong may be warned, and as glad tidings to the doers of good.

Assuredly they who say, "Our Lord is God" and take the straight way to Him—no fear shall come on them, neither shall they grieve.

These shall be the inmates of Paradise to remain therein for ever,—the recompense of their deeds! (Q. 46 : 11-13)

Had we made it a Koran in a foreign tongue, they had surely said, "Unless its verses be made clear ... What! in a foreign tongue? and the people Arabian? Say: It is to those who believe a guide and a healing; but as to those who believe not, there is a thickness in their ears, and to them it is a blindness: They are like those who are called to from afar. (Q. 41 : 44)

It is thus moreover that we have revealed to thee an Arabic Koran, that thou mayest warn the mother city and all around it. (Q. 42 : 5)

We have made it an Arabic Koran that ye may understand. (Q. 43 : 2)

We have made this Koran easy for thee in thine own tongue, that they may take the warning. (Q. 44 : 58)

That this verily is the word of an illustrious messenger!

And that it is not the word of a poet—how little do ye believe!

Neither is it the word of a soothsayer (Kahin)—how little do ye receive warning!

It is a revelation from the Lord of the worlds.

(Q. 60 : 40-43)

That this is the word of illustrious Messenger,
Endued with power, influence with the Lord of the Throne,
Obeyed there by Angels, faithful to his trust,
And your compatriot is not one possessed by djinn.

(Q. 81 : 19-22)

And to thee we have sent down the Book of the Koran with truth, confirmatory of previous Scriptures, and their safeguard. Judge therefore between them by what God hath sent down, and, follow not their desires by deserting the truth which hath come unto thee. To every one of you have we given a rule and a beaten track. And if God had pleased He had surely made you all one people; but He would test you by what He hath given to each. Be emulous, then, in good deeds. To God shall ye all return, and He will tell you concerning the subjects of your disputes. (Q. 5:52-53)

NO COMPULSION IN RELIGION.

There is no compulsion in religion. (Q. 2:256)

But if thy Lord had pleased, verily all who are in the earth would have believed together. What! wilt thou compel men to become believers? (Q. 10:99)

Follow thou that which hath been revealed to thee by thy Lord: there is no God but He! and withdraw from those who join other Gods with Him.

Had God pleased, they had not joined other Gods with Him: and we have not made thee keeper over them, neither art thou a guardian over them.

Revile not those whom they call on beside God, lest they in their ignorance, dispitefully revile Him.

Thus have we planned out their actions for every people; then shall they return to their Lord, and He will declare to them what those actions have been. (Q. 6:106-108)

Say: O ye unbelivers! *

I worship not that which ye worship,

* The term 'Kafar' (Unbeliever) is derived from the root 'Kafara' which means (1) to cover. (2) to deny, (3) to show ingratitude. So 'Kafar' means he who hides a thing, or denies it, or is ungrateful to God, or who does not thank God for what He has provided for man. 'Kafar' also means a peasant, since he covers the seed. The term is used in one or other of these several senses. Generally, it is used to mean one who did not listen to Prophet Muhammad in his time or did not recognise the Supreme Being who had provided one and all the good things of life.

In verses Q. 14:32-34 and Q. 17:67 (as numbered in Pickthal's Translation) the term 'Kafar' is used in the sense of 'ungrateful' and applied to all humanity.

The term is also applied to the Jews of the Prophet's time (Q. 17:8) since they had neglected their scripture, the Torah. In verse (Q. 21:94), the term is applied to God Himself since He recognises or rewards or does not hide one's good work. The same idea is conveyed in the Gita (2:40). In (Q. 29:7) the term means to blot out, to remit, to cover sins. In (Q. 4:150-151), it is pointed out that the real kafars are those who recognise certain messengers of God and deny others.

And ye do not worship that which I worship;
I shall never worship that which ye worship,
Neither will ye worship that which I worship.
To you be the recompence of what ye do; to me the recompence of what I do. (Q. 109 : 1-7)

The last two passages were delivered at a time when the non-Muslims in Mecca were engaged in a bitter fight with the followers of the Prophet.

God doth not forbid you to deal with kindness and fairness toward those who have not made war upon you on account of your religion, or driven you forth from your homes; for god loveth those who act with fairness.

Only doth God forbid you to make friends of those who on account of your religion, have warred against you, and have driven you forth from your homes, and have aided those who drove you forth: and whoever maketh friends of them are wrong-doers. (Q. 6 : 8-9)

Tell the believers to pardon those who hope not for the days of God in which He purposeth to reward men according to their deeds.

He who doth that which is right, doth it so to his own behoof; and whoso doth evil, doth it to his own hurt. Hereafter, to your Lord shall ye be brought back. (Q. 45 : 13, 14)

GOD IS ALL-PERVADING.

The East and the West is God's: therefore, whichever way ye turn, there is the face of God: Truly God is All-pervading and All-knowing". (Q. 2 : 109)

For full 13 years of His Prophetic mission, Muhammad lived and preached in Mecca. During this period no fixed direction had been prescribed to turn to in daily prayer. On reaching Madina, he used to turn towards Jerusalem for a while, even as the Jews and the Christians did. But after a stay of 16 months there, he began to turn to the South, toward the seat of Kaaba at Mecca. A few people raised objection to this change. The following Qur'ānic verse was then delivered in answer:

The foolish ones will say: "What hath turned them from the Kebla which they used?" Say: The East and the West are God's. He guideth whom he will into the right path. (Q. 2: 136)

There is no piety in turning your faces towards the east or west, but he is pious who believeth in God, and the last day, and the angels, and the scriptures, and the prophets, who for the love of God disburseth his wealth to his kindred, and to the orphans, and the needy and the wayfarer, and those who ask, and for ransoming; who observeth prayer, and payeth the legal alms, and who is of those who are faithful to their engagements when they have engaged in them, and patient under ills and hardships and in time of trouble; these are they who are just and these are they who fear the Lord." (Q. 2: 172)

There is a hilly place near Medina by name Quba. The Prophet and his followers had taken rest in their retreat from Mecca to Medina. Soon a small mosque was erected for the use of the Muslims of the locality. A little time thereafter, several Muslims of the place erected another mosque of their own. Those who had built this mosque came to the Prophet and requested him to come to Quba and offer prayer at this new mosque. Dissension among the Muslims of the place was apprehended. The Prophet was apprised of the risk by the verse revealed at the time:

"The mosque which is likely to create dissensions among the believers is not the place where the prophet should stand for prayer." (Q. 9: 107)

The Prophet therefore refused to accede to the request. Under his orders, the new mosque was demolished.

"And every one hath a goal to which he turneth: so hasten emulously after good: Wherever ye be, God will one day bring you all together: verily, God is able to do all things." (Q. 2:143)

PROPHET MUHAMMED AND MIRACLES

"Say: I am no apostle of new doctrines; neither know I what will be done with me or you. Only what is revealed to me do I follow, and I am only charged to warn openly." (Q. 46: 8)

"Muhammad is no more than an apostle; other apostles have already passed away before him: if he die, therefore, or be slain, will ye turn upon your heels?" (Q. 3: 138)

The above was the verse which the first Khalif Abu Bakr, recited to the people of Medina on the day the Prophet passed away.

"Say: I say not to you, "In my possession are the treasures of God:" neither say, "I know things secret"; neither do I say to you, "Verily, I am an angel": Only what is revealed to me do I follow." (Q. 6: 50)

"With their most solemn oath have they sworn by God, that if a sign come unto them they will certainly believe it; Say: Signs are in the power of God alone". (Q. 6: 109)

"And they say, "By no means will we believe on thee till thou cause a fountain to gush forth for us form the earth."

"Or, till thou have a garden of palm-trees and grapes, and thou cause forth gushing rivers to gush forth in its midst."

"Or thou make the heaven to fall on us, as thou hast given out, in pieces; or thou bring God and the angels to vouch for thee."

"Or thou have a house of gold; or thou mount up into Heaven; nor will we believe in thy mounting up, till thou send down to us a book which we may read." Say:

"Praise be to my Lord! Am I more than a man, an apostle.?" (Q. 17: 92-96)

"And they say, "Unless a sign be sent down to him from his Lord......" Say: signs are in the power of God alone. I am only a plain-speaking warner." (Q. 29: 49)

"Marvel ye that a warning should come to you from your Lord through one of yourselves, that he may warn you, and that ye may fear for yourselves, and that haply ye may find mercy?" (Q. 29: 49)

"Say: I have no control over what may be helpful or hurtful to me, but as God willeth. Had I the knowledge of His secrets, I should revel in the good, and evil should not touch me. But I am only a warner, and an announcer of good tidings to those who believe" (Q. 7: 188)

"But say: "The hidden is only with God: wait therefore: I truly will be with you among those who wait."

(Q. 10: 21)

"Say: In sooth I am only a man like you. It hath been revealed to me that your God is one only God: let him then who hopeth to meet his Lord work a righteous work: nor let him give any creature a share in the worship of his Lord." (Q. 18: 110)

"Say: I am only a man like you. It is revealed to me that your God is one God: go straight then to Him, and implore his pardon." (Q. 41: 5)

"Only this has been revealed to me that I am to be a plain warner." (Q. 38: 70)

PERMISSION TO TAKE UP ARMS

The first 13 years of the Prophet's mission were years of endless suffering at the hands of the Meccans. The verses that were delivered during these years enjoined on the Prophet to return good for evil, and exercise patience with strict adherence to truth. By way of relief, the Prophet sought asylum at Medina along with some of his followers. The Meccans would not give him rest even there. They waged war against him. It was for the first time that the following verses were delivered calling upon the Prophet to defend himself against his oppressors.

"Permission to take up arms is given to those on whom war is made, beause they have suffered outrages: and verily, God is well able to succour them."

"Those who have been driven forth from their homes wrongfully, only beacause they say "Our Lord is the God." And if God had not repelled some men by others, cloisters and churches, and oratories and mosques, wherein the name of God is ever commemorated would surely have been destroyed.

And him who helpeth, God will surely help: for God is right Strong, Mighty:

"Those who, if we establish them in this land, will observe prayer, and pay the poor-due and enjoin what is right, and forbid what is evil. And the final issue of all things is unto God." (Q. 22: 39-42)

Notwithstanding this permission to fight the aggressors, the followers of the Prophet were reluctant to take up arms, as the opposing forces were composed of their own kith and kin. It is in such a situation that the following verses were delivered:

> War is prescribed to you: but from this ye are averse. Yet haply ye are averse from a thing, though it be good for you, and haply ye love a thing though it be bad for you: And God knoweth; but ye, ye know not.
>
> (Q. 2:212-213)
>
> Let those then fight on the path of God, who barter this present life for that which is to come; for whoever fighteth on God's path, whether he be slain or conquer, we will in the end give him a great reward.
>
> But what hath come to you that ye fight not on the path of God, and for the weak among men, women, and children, who say, "O our Lord! bring us forth from this city whose inhabitants are oppressors; give us a champion from thy presence; and give us from thy presence a defender." (Q. 4:76-78)
>
> Fight therefore, on God's path: lay not burdens on any but thyself; and stir up the faithful. The might of the infidles haply will God restrain, for God is the stronger in prowess, and the stronger to punish.
>
> He who shall mediate between men for a good purpose shall be the gainer by it. But he who shall mediate with an evil mediation shall reap the fruit of it. And God keepeth watch over everything.
>
> If ye are greeted with a greeting, then greet ye with a better greeting, or at least return it; God taketh count of all things.
>
> God! there is no god but he! He will certainly assemble you on the day of resurrection. There is no doubt of it. And whose word is more true than God's? (Q. 4: 86-89)
>
> Except those who shall seek an asylum among your allies, and those who come over to you — their hearts forbidding them to make war on you, or to make war on their own people, Had God pleased, he would have given them power gainst you, and they would have made war upon you! But, if they depart from you, and make not war against you and offer you peace then God alloweth you no occasion against them. (Q. 4:92)

O believers ! when ye go forth to the fight for the cause of God, be discerning, and say not to every one who meeteth you with a greeting, "Thou are not a believer" in your greed after the chance good things of this present life ! With God are abundant spoils. Such hath been your wont in times past ; but God hath been gracious to you. Be discerning, then, for God well knoweth what ye do. (Q. 4 : 96)

And if they incline to peace, incline thou also to it, and trust in Allāh. Lo ! He, even He, is the Hearer, the Knower.

And if they would deceive thee, then lo ! Allāh is sufficient for thee. He it is who supporteth thee with His help and with the believers.

And (as for the believers) hath attuned their hearts. If thou hadst spent all that is in the earth, thou couldst not have attuned their hearts, but Allāh hath attuned them. Lo ! He is Mighty, Wise.

O Prophet ! Allah is sufficient for thee and those who follow thee of the believers. (Q. 8 : 61-64)

O ye who believe ! when ye meet the marshalled hosts of the infidels turn not your backs to them :

Whoso shall turn his back to them on that day, unless they turn aside to fight or to rally to some other troop, shall incur wrath from God : Hell shall be his abode and wretched the journey thither ! (Q. 8 : 15-16)

And fight for the cause of God against those who fight against you : but commit not the injustice of attacking them first : God loveth not such injustice.

And kill them wherever ye shall find them, and eject them from whatever place they have ejected you ; for civil discord is worse than carnage : yet attack them not at the sacred Mosque, unless they attack you therein ; but if they attack you, slay them. Such the reward of the infidels.

But If they desist, then verily God is Gracious, Merciful.

Fight therefore against them until there be no more civil discord, and the only worship be that of God : but if they desist, then let there be no hostility save against the wicked.

The sacred month and sacred precincts are under the safeguard of reprisals : whoever offereth violence to you, offer ye the like violence to him and fear God, and know that God is with those who fear Him.

Give freely for the cause of God, and throw not yourselves with your own hands into ruin; and do good, for God loveth those who do good. (Q. 2: 186-191)

If two bodies of the faithful are at war, then make ye peace between them: and if the one of them wrong the other, fight against that party which doth the wrong, until they come back to the precepts of God: if they come back, make peace between them with fairness, and act impartially, God loveth those who act with impartiality.

(Q. 49:9)

These are the verses of the Qur'ān which afford permission to take up arms in self-defence both against Muslims and Non-Muslims.

It was a custom in the past both with the Arabs and the people of the countries adjoining Arabia to kill or enslave those of the enemy forces who were captured. The Qur'ān abolished this custom and issued the following commandment.

And afterwards let there either be free dismissals or ransomings, till the war hath laid down its burdens.

(Q. 47: 5)

After the termination of war it was not permitted to keep any captives in prison.

Thus do. Were such the pleasure of God, He could Himself take vengeance upon them: but He would rather prove the one of you by the other. And whoso fight for the cause of God, their works he will not suffer to miscarry.

(Q 47:5)

Following this principle, the Prophet set free those captured in warfare with or without receiving ransom. After the battle of Badar, he set free 70 captives on receiving a nominal ransom. But those who were literate and were poor were each asked- in lieu of ransom, to teach reading and writing 10 of his followers in Madina for a time and then leave for their homes.

On one occasion he set free one hundred families of the tribe of Mustalaq, and on another occasion he set free 6,000 captives of the tribe of Hawan without demanding any ransom.

The old practice of trading in slaves was considerably reduced by the observance of such a procedure.

PROPAGATION OF FAITH*

> And if he summon them to 'the guidance' they hear you not: thou seest them look towards thee but they do not see!
>
> Make the best of things; and enjoin what is just, and withdraw from the ignorant:
>
> (Q. 7 : 197-198)
>
> If any one of those who join gods with God ask any asylum of thee, grant him an asylum, that he may hear the Word of God. and then let him reach his place of safety. This, for that they are people devoid of knowledge.
>
> (Q. 9 : 6)
>
> And if they charge thee with imposture, then say: My work for me, and your work for you! Ye are clear of that which I do, and I am clear of that which ye do.
>
> And some of them lend a ready ear to thee: But wilt thou make the deaf to hear even though they understand not?
>
> And some of them look at thee: But wilt thou guide the blind even though they see not?
>
> Verily, God will not wrong men in aught, but men will wrong themselves. (Q. 10 : 42-45)
>
> Summon thou to the way of thy Lord with wisdom and with kindly warning: dispute with them in the kindest manner: thy Lord best knoweth those who stray from his way, and He best knoweth those who have yielded to his guidance.
>
> If ye make reprisals, then make them to the same extent that ye were injured: But if ye can endure patiently, best will it be for the patiently enduring.
>
> Endure then with patience. But thy patient endurance must be sought in none but God. And be not grieved about the infidels, and be not troubled at their devices; for God is with those who fear him and do good deeds.
>
> (Q. 16 : 126-128)

*There are other verses in the Qur'ān which present the subject in a clearer light.

DOING GOOD TO OTHERS.

Thy Lord hath ordained that ye worship none but Him; and, kindness to your parents, whether one or both of them attain to old age with thee: and say not to them, "Fie!" neither reproach them; but speak to them both with respectful speech;

And defer humbly to them out of tenderness, and say "Lord, have compassion on them both, even as they reared me when I was little."

Your Lord well knoweth what is in your souls; he knoweth whether ye be righteous:

And gracious is He to those who return to Him.

And to him who is of kin render his due, and also to the poor and to the wayfarer: yet waste not wastefully.

(Q. 17: 24-28)

Kill not your children for fear of want: for them and for you will we provide. Verily, the killing them is a great wickedness.

Have nought to do with adultery: for it is a foul thing and an evil way: (Q. 17: 33-34)

And touch not the substance of the orphan, unless in an upright way, till he attain his age of strength: And perform your covenant; verily the covenant shall be enquired of:

And give full measure when you measure, and weigh with just balance. This will be better, and fairest for settlement:

And follow not that of which thou hast no knowledge because the hearing and the sight and the heart,—each of these shall be enquired of:

And walk not proudly on the earth, for thou canst not cleave the earth, neither shalt thou reach to the mountains in height;

All this is evil; odious to thy Lord. (Q. 17: 36-40)

For this cause have we ordained to the children of Israel that he who slayeth any one, unless it be a person guilty of manslaughter, or of spreading disorders in the land, shall be as though he had slain all mankind; but that he who saveth a life, shall be as though he had saved all mankind alive. (Q. 5: 35)

Say: Come, I will rehearse what your Lord hath made binding on you — that ye assign not aught to Him as partner; and that ye be good to your parents; and that ye slay not your children, because of poverty: for them and for you will we provide: and that ye come not near to pollutions, outward or inward, and that ye slay not anyone whom God hath forbidden you, unless for a just cause. This hath he enjoined on you, to the intent that ye may understand.

And come not nigh to the substance of the orphan, but to improve it, until he come of age: and use a full measure and a just balance: We will not task a soul beyond its ability. And when ye give judgement, observe justice, even though it be the affair of a kinsman, and fulfil the covenant of God. This hath God enjoined you for your monition —

And, "this is my right way." Follow it then; and follow not other paths lest ye be scattered from His path. This hath he enjoined you, that ye may fear Him.

(Q. 6: 152-154)

And clothe not the truth with falsehood, and hide not the truth when ye know it:

And observe prayer and pay the legal impost, and bow down with those who bow.

Will ye enjoin what is right upon others, and forget yourselves? Yet ye read the Book: will ye not understand?

And seek help with patience and prayer: a hard duty indeed is this but not to the humble. (Q. 2: 39-42)

Consume not your wealth among yourselves in vain things, nor present it to judges that ye may consume a part of other men's wealth unjustly, while ye know the sin which ye commit. (Q. 2: 184)

Give freely for the cause of God, and throw not yourselves with your own hands into ruin; and do good for God loveth those who do good. (Q. 2: 192)

They will ask thee concerning wine and games of chance. Say: In both is great sin, and advantage also, to men; but their sin is greater than their advantage. (Q. 2: 216)

O Believers! surely, wine and games of chance, and statues, and the divining arrows, are an abomination of Satan's work! Avoid them, that ye may prosper. (Q. 5: 93)

A kind speech and forgiveness is bether than alms followed by injury, God is Rich, Clement.

O ye who believe! make not your alms void by reproaches and injury, like him who spendeth his substance to be seen of men, and believeth not in God and in the latter day. The likeness of such an one is that of a rock with a thin soil upon it, on which a heavy rain falleth but leaveth it hard: No profit from their works shall they be able to gain; for God guideth not the unbelieving people. (Q. 2:265-66)

O ye who believe! bestow alms of the good things which ye have acquired, and of that which we have brought forth for you out of the earth, and choose not the bad for almsgiving. (Q. 2:269)

Give ye your alms openly? it is well. Do ye conceal them and give them to the poor? This, too will be of advantage to you, and will do away your sins: and God is cognisant of your actions. (Q. 2:273)

God hath forbidden usury. (Q. 2:76)

O ye who believe! devour not usury, doubling it again and again! But fear God, that ye may prosper. (Q. 3:125)

Say: I betake me for refuge to the Lord of the Day-Break against the mischief of the envier when he envieth. (Q. 113:5)

Ye shall never attain to goodness till ye give alms of that which ye love; and whatever ye give, of a truth God knoweth it. (Q. 3:86)

And vie in haste for pardon from your Lord, and a Paradise, vast as the Heavens and the Earth, prepared for the God-fearing,

Who give alms, alike in prosperity and in success, and who master their anger, and forgive others! God loveth the doers of good. (Q. 3:127-28)

Verily they who swallow the substance of the orphan wrongfully, shall swallow down only fire into their bellies; and shall burn in the flame! (Q. 4:11)

God desireth thus to turn him unto you: but they who follow their own lusts, desire that with great swerving should ye swerve! God desireth to make your burden light: for man hath been created weak. (Q. 4:32)

Covet not the gifts by which God hath raised some of you above others. The men shall have a portion according to their deserts, and the women a portion according to their deserts. Of God, therefore, ask his gifts. Verily, God hath knowledge of all things. (Q. 4 : 36)

Worship God, and join not aught with Him in worship. Be good to parents, and to kindred, and to orphans, and to the poor, and to a neighbour, whether kinsman or new-comer, and to a fellow traveller, and to the wayfarer, and to the slaves whom your right hands hold; verily, God loveth not the proud, the vain boaster. (Q. 4 : 40)

O ye who believe! stand fast to justice, when ye bear witness before God, though it be against yourselves, or your parents, or your kindred, whether the party be rich or poor. God is nearer than you to both. Therefore follow not passion, lest ye swerve from truth. And of ye wrest your testimony or stand aloof, God verily is well aware of what ye do. (Q. 4 : 134)

O believers! stand up as witnesses for God by righteousness: and let not ill-will at any, induce you not to act uprightly. Next will this be to the fear of God. And fear ye God: verily, God is apprised of what ye do. (Q. 5 : 11)

For when the birth of a daughter is announced to any one of them, dark shadows settle on his face, and he is said:

He hideth him from the people because of the ill tidings: shall he keep it with disgrace or bury it in the dust? Are not their judgments wrong? (Q. 16 : 60-61)

O Believers! of a truth, many of the teachers and monks do devour man's substance in vanity, and turn them from the way of God. But wto those who treasure up gold and silver and expend it not in the way of God announce tidings of a grievous torment. (Q. 9 : 34)

Except those who endure with patience and do the things that are right: these doth pardon await and a great reward. (Q. 11 : 15)

Verily God enjoineth justice and the doing of good and gifts to kindred; and he forbiddeth wickedness and wrong and oppression. He warneth you that haply ye may be mindful.

Be faithful in the covenant of God when ye have covenanted, and break not your oaths after ye have pledged them: for now have ye made God to stand surety for you. Verily, God hath knowledge of what ye do.

And because you are a more numerous people, than some other people, be not like her who unravelleth the thread which she had strongly spun, by taking your oaths with mutual perfidy. God is making trial of you in this: and in the day of resurrection he will assuredly clear up to you that concerning which ye are now at variance.

Had God pleased, He could have made you one people: but He causeth whom He will to err, and whom He will He guideth: and ye shall assuredly be called to account for your doings.

Therefore take not your oaths with mutual fraud, lest your foot slip after it hath been firmly fixed, and ye taste of evil because ye have turned others aside from the way of God, and great be your punishment.

And barter not the covenant of God for a mean price: for with God is that which is better for you, if ye do but understand.

All that is with you passeth away, but that which is with God abideth. With a reward meet for their best deeds will we surely recompense those who have patiently endured.

Whoso doeth that which is right, whether male or female, if a believer, him will we surely quicken to a happy life, and recompense them with a reward meet for their best deeds. (Q. 16:92-99)

Wealth and children are the adornment of this present life: but good works, which are lasting, are better in the sight of thy Lord as to recompense, and better as to hope. (Q. 18:44)

By no means can their flesh reach unto God, neither their blood; but piety on your part reacheth Him. Thus hath He subjected them to you, that ye might magnify God for His guidance: moreover, announce to those who do good deeds. (Q. 22:38)

The whore and the whoremonger — scourge each of them with an hundred stripes; and let not compassion keep you from carrying out the sentence of God, if ye believe in God and the last day: And let some of the faithful witness their chastisement. (Q. 24:2)

And the servants of the God of Mercy are they who walk upon the Earth softly; and when the ignorant address them, they reply, "Peace!". (Q. 25:64)

O my son! observe prayer, and enjoin the right and forbid the wrong, and be patient under whatever shall betide thee! for this is a bounden duty.

And distort not thy face at men; nor walk thou loftily on the earth; for God loveth no arrogant vain-glorious one.

But let thy pace be middling; and lower thy voice; for the least pleasing of voices is surely the voice of asses. (Q. 31:16-18)

Think men that when they say, "We believe", they shall be let alone and not be put to proof?

Think they who work evil that they shall escape Us? Ill do they judge.

And those who shall have believed and done the things that are right, we will surely give them an entering in among the just. (Q. 29:2, 4 and 9)

Moreover, we have enjoined on man to shew kindness to his parents. With pain his mother beareth him; with pain she bringeth him forth: and his bearing and his weaning is thirty months; until when he attaineth his strength, and attaineth to forty years, he saith, "O my God! stir me up to be grateful for thy favours wherewith thou hast favoured me and my parents, and to do good works which shall please thee: and proposer me in my offspring: for to thee am I turned, and am resigned to thy will (as a Muslim). (Q. 46:15)

O Believers: let not men laugh men to scorn who haply may be better than themselves; neither let women laugh women to scorn who may haply be better than themselves! Neither defame one another, nor call one another by nicknames. Bad is it to be called wicked after having professed the faith: and who repent not of this are doers of wrong.

O Believers! avoid frequent suspicions, for some suspicions are a crime; and pry not: neither let the one of you traduce another in his absence. Would any one of you like to eat the flesh of his dead brother? Surely ye would loathe it. And fear ye God: for God is Ready to turn, Merciful.

O men! verily, we have created you of a male and a female; and we have divided you into peoples and tribes that ye might have knowledge one of another. Truly, the most worthy of honour in the sight of God is he who feareth Him most. Verily, God is Knowing Cognisant. (Q. 49: 11-13)

Lest ye distress yourselves if good things escape you, and be over joyous for what falleth to your share. God loveth not the presumptuos, the boaster. (Q. 57-23)

But as to him who shall have feared the majesty of his Lord, and shall have refrained his soul from lust.

Verily, Paradise—that shall be his dwelling-place.

(Q. 79: 40-41)

Once, a blind man, by name Abdullah, came to the Prophet and asked to hear the Qur'ān. At the time, the Prophet was engaged in conversation with a leader of the tribe of Quraish. He did not like the blind man's interruption, and turned away from him. Came then the Revelation to him in the following admonishing terms:—

He frowned, and he turned his back,
Because the blind man came to him!
But what assured thee that he would not be cleansed by the Faith,
Or be warned, and the warning profit him?
As to whim who is free from need—
To him thou wast all attention:
Yet is it not thy concern if he be not cleansed:
But as to him who cometh to thee in earnest,
And full of fears—
Him dost thou neglect.
Nay; but it (the Koran) is a warning. (Q. 80: 1-11)

It is stated in the traditions that the Prophet felt sad over what he had done. Thereafter he treated the blind man with the utmost respect; so much so, that he twice made him Governor of Medina.

What thinkest thou of him who treateth our RELIGION as a lie?

He it is who thruseth away the orphan,
And stirreth not others up to feed the poor.
Woe to those who pray,
But in their prayer are careless;
Who make a shew of devotion,
But refuse help to the needy. (Q. 102 : 1-8)

Woe to those who stint the measure:
Who when they take by measure from others, exact the full;
But when they mete to them or weight to them, minish—
(Q. 83 : 1-3)

And the Heaven, He hath reared it on high, and hath appointed the balance;
That in the balance ye should not transgress.
Weigh therefore with fairness, and scant not the balance.
(Q. 55 : 7-9)

What! have we not made him eyes,
And tongue, and lips,
And guided him to the two highways?
Yet he attempted not the Steep
And who shall teach thee what the steep is?
It is to ransom the captive,
Or to feed in the day of famine,
The orphan who is near of kin, or the poor that lieth in the dust;
Beside this, to be of those who believe and enjoin steadfastness on each other, and enjoin compassion on each other.
These shall be the people of the right hand:
While they who disbelieve our signs,
Shall be the people of the left.
Around them the fire shall close. (Q. 90 : 8-20)

As to the orphan therefore wrong him not;
And as to him that asketh of thee, chide him not away
And as for the favours of thy Lord tell them abroad.
(Q. 93 : 9-11)

I swear by the declining day!
Verily, man's lot is cast amid destruction,
Save those who believe and do the things which be right, and enjoin truth and enjoin steadfastness on each other.
(Q. 103 : 1-3)

Yet was not aught enjoined on them but to worship God in perfect sincerity, being upright, and observe prayer and the poor-rate; and this is the right religion. (Q. 98 : 5)

What thinkest thou of him who belieth religion?
He it is who thrusteth away the orphan,
And stirreth not others up to feed the poor.
Woe to those who pray,
But in their prayer are careless;
Who make a shew of devotion.
But refuse help to the needy. (Q. 107:1, 7)

RETURN GOOD FOR EVIL.

Relate to them exactly the story of the sons of Adam when they each offered an offering; accepted from the one of them, and not accepted from the other. The one said, "I will surely slay thee". Said the other, "God only accepted from those that fear Him."

"Even if thou stretch forth thine hand against me to slay me, I will not stretch forth my hand against thee to slay thee. Truly I fear God the Lord of the Worlds. (Q. 5:30-31)

And therein have we enacted for them, "Life for life, and eye for eye, and nose for nose, and ear for ear, and tooth for tooth, and for wounds retaliation:" — Whoso shall forego it shall have therein the expiation of his sin. (Q. 5:49)

And let not ill-will at those who would have kept you from the sacred mosque lead you to transgress, but rather be helpful to one another according to goodness and piety, but be not helpful for evil and malice: and fear ye God. (Q. 5:3)

And who, from, desire to see the face of their Lord, are constant amid trials, and observe prayer and give alms in secret and openly, out of what we have bestowed upon them, and turn aside evil by good: for there is the recompense of that abode. (Q. 13:22)

If ye make reprisals, then make them to the same extent that ye were injured: but ye can endure patiently, best will it be for the patiently enduring.

Endure than with patience. But thy patient endurance must be sought in none but God. And be not grieved about the infidels, and be not troubled at their devices; for God is with those who fear him and do good deeds. (Q. 16:127-128)

Moreover good and evil are not to be treated as the same thing. Turn away evil by what is better, and lo! he between whom and thyself was enmity, shall be as though he were a warm friend.

But none attain to this save men steadfast in patience, and none attain to it except the most highly favoured.

(Q. 41 : 34-35)

Yet let the recompence of evil be only alike evil - but he who forgiveth and is reconciled, shall be rewarded by God himself; for He loveth not those who act unjustly.

And there shall be no way open against those who, after being wronged, avenge themselves;

But there shall be a way open against those who unjustly wrong others, and act insolently on the earth in disregard of justice. These! a grievous punishment doth await them.

And whoso beareth wrongs with patience and forgiveth;— this verily is a high resolve. (Q. 42 : 38-41)

Turn aside evil with that which is better: we best know what they utter against thee. (Q. 23 : 98)

CONCERNING WOMEN

The relationship that should subsist between man and woman is the subject of many verses in the Qur'ān. The advice and directions embodied therein speedily wrought reformation in the Arab social life. Even as stated in 'Narva Smrithi' of the Hindus that women are the field of cultivation and men have to sow seeds therein. so in the Qur'ān it is stated that the function of women is not to satisfy merely the desire of men but to perpetuate the race of men and bring up their progeny.

Your wives are your field: go in, therefore, to your field as ye will; but do first some act for your souls' good: and fear ye God, and know that ye must meet Him;

(Q. 2 : 223)

Prior to the advent of the Prophet, the Arab women enjoyed no rights. They had absolutely no share in the property left behind by their parents. Their position in society was that of mere chattel or marketable commodity. The Qur'ān came to set things right by proclaiming:

> Even as men have rights over women, even so women have rights over men. (Q. 2:228)
>
> And women have rights similar to those against them in a just manner. (Q. 2:228)
>
> They are an apparel for you, and you are an apparel for them. (Q. 2:187)

The Qur'ān repeatedly asks men to treat well their womenfolk, to behave justly with them and to protect their property. It makes it obligatory on the part of men not to appropriate for their own use anything that belongs to their wives or anything that they might have given them as gifts. (Q. 2:229)

Prior to the Qur'ān, a woman was not entitled to any share in the property left behind by either father, brother, husband or any relation. The Qur'ān put a stop to this custom and declared:

> Men ought to have a part of what their parents and kindred leave: and women a part of what their parents and kindered leave: whether it be little or much, let them have a stated portion. (Q. 4:8)

Likewise, young children had previously no right of succession to the property of their parents or any of their relations, since the general rule observed among them was that "any one who could not throw aright his javeline while attacking another was not fitted to receive any share in any property." This was natural in a society perennially engaged in tribal feuds or internecine warfare. TheQur'ān fixes the share of every one who survives.

> Verily they who swallow the substance of the orphan wrongfully, shall swallow down only fire into their bellies, and shall burn in the flame! (Q. 4:11)
>
> They will consult thee. Say: God instructeth you as to distant kindred.
>
> If a man die childless, but have a sister, half what he shall have shall be her's and if she die childless he shall be her heir. But if there be two sisters two-third parts of what he shall have shall be theirs; and if there be both brothers and sisters, the male shall have the portion of two females.

> God teacheth you plainly, that ye err not! God knoweth all things. (Q. 4:177)

In matters of marriage, there was no definite rule prohibiting one to marry particular relations of his. In fact, after the death of one's father, his widows became the property of his son and he could makc a free use of any one of them he liked. The Qur'ān put a stop to this reprehensible practice and laid down specific rules in respect of prohibitions.

> And marry not women whom your fathers have married: for this is a shame, and hateful, and an evil way: (Q. 4:26)

> Forbidden to you are your mothers, and your daughters, and your sisters, and your aunts, both on the father and mother's side, and your nieces on the brother and sister's side, and your foster-mothers, and your foster-sisters, and the mothers of your wives, and your step-daughters who are your wards, born of your wives to whom ye have gone in: (but if ye have not gone in unto them, it shall be no sin in you to marry them;) and the wives of your sons who proceed out of your loins; and ye may not have two sisters; except where it is already done. Verily. God is Indulgent, Merciful! (Q.4:27)

The Qur'ān regarded it illegal and sinful to cohabit with any woman except his own wedded wife, no matter whether it be a slave woman,

> And whoever of you is not rich enough to marry free believing women, then let him marry such of your believing maidens as have fallan into your hands as slaves; God well knoweth your truth. You are sprung the one from the other. Marry them, then, with the leave of their masters, and give them a fair dower: but let them be chaste and free from fornication, and not entertainers of lovers. (Q. 4:29)

Women were permitted to work on their own and to own property of their own and exercise complete rights over what they have earned or possessed.

> For men is the benefit of what they earn; and for women is the benefit of what they earn. (Q. 4:32)

Nevertheless, it was made obligatory on men to provide means of sustenance to womenfolk and children and to look after them in every respect, and it was made obligatory on women to feed their infants for full two years after their birth (Q. 2 : 232-233, 4 : 34)

Should there be any quarrels between man and woman, the Qur'ānic injunction was:

> And if ye fear a breach between man and wife, then send a judge chosen from his family and a judge chosen from her family: if they are desirous of agreement, God will effect a reconciliation between them: Verily, God is Knowing, Apprised of all! (Q. 4 : 39)
>
> And if a wife fear ill usage or aversion on the part of her husband, then shall it be no fault in them if they can agree with mutual agreement, for agreement is best. (Q. 4 : 127)

Should there still be no compromise reached between the two, the Qur'ān under special circumstances and on exacting conditions gives permission for divorce. But it stipulates that no woman could be divorced during the period of pregnancy and that adequate financial provision should be made for the divorced woman before she is divorced.

> As to such of your wives as have no hope of the recurrence of their times, if ye have doubts in regard to them, then reckon three months, and let the same be the term of those who have not yet had them. And as to those who are with child, their period shall be until they are delivered of their burden. God will make His command easy to him who feareth Him. (Q. 65 : 4)
>
> And for the divorced let there be a fair provision. This is a duty on those who fear God. (Q. 2 : 242)

The duty of man is to treat his wife with tenderness and justice, and should he find it necessary to separate, he should do so in mutual goodwill.

> But when ye divorce women, and the time for sending them away is come either retain with generosity, or put them away with generosity: but retain them not by constraint so as to be unjust towards them. He who doth so, doth

> in fact injure himself. And make not the signs of God a jest; but remember God's favour toward you, and the Book and the Wisdom which He hath sent down to you for your warning, and fear God, and know that God's knowledge embraceth everything. (Q. 2 : 231)

Even as the man has right to divorce his wife, the woman has the right to divorce her husband. But the well known saying of the Prophet: "Of the things permitted, the most hated by God is divorce. (Abu Dawood)".

Of a couple. should one die, the other is permitted to remarry (Q. 2: 234). Man is permitted to marry more than one, but not more than four. But, be it noted, that this permission was given soon after the battle of Uhad A great many men among the followers of the Prophet had been killed in this battle, so much so, that the question of providing a vast number of widows and orphans had to be solved. The widowed women could by themselves make no provision for their orphaned children. And then, the prospect stared hard in the face that further battles with the enemy were to follow, adding to the number of widows and orphans in the Muslim camp. It was in such circumstances that the order to have more than one and not more than four wives was issued (Q. 4: 3)

But it was clearly observed by the Qur'ān that it was not possible to look, with an equal eye, on all the four, and that normally, therefore, it would be better to have only one wife (Q. 4 : 3, 129). It was under such an exceptional situation that the order of having more than one wife had been delivered; but the same order records a preferential leaning for only one.

The Qur'ān regards the misbehaviour on the part of both men and women as a heineous sin. The punishment prescribed for fornication was 100 stripes in public. Men with clean lives were prohibited to marry women with unclelan lives. At the same time, any wrongful accusation of women was punishable by 80 stripes (24 : 1-4). The universal prayer that every one was asked to utter forth was to seek protection of God from the clutches of Satan, from filthy talk and sexual misbehaviour and to seek Divine aid for self-purification (24 : 21 etc). Good life was enjoined on both the married and the unmarried, and on slaves and slave owners alike (Q. 29 . 32-33).

The attitude of the Qur'ān towards what is called Parda is contained in the following verses :

> O Prophet! Tell thy wives and thy daughters and the women of the believers to draw their cloaks close round them (when they go abroad). That will be better, so that they may be recognised and not annoyed. (Q. 33-59)
>
> Tell the believing men to lower their gaze and be modest. That is purer for them. Lo! Allāh is Aware of what they do.
>
> And tell the believing women to lower their gaze and be modest, and to display of their adornment only that which is apparent, and to draw their veils over their bosoms, and not to reveal their adornment save to their own husbands or fathers or husbands' fathers, or their sons or their husbands' sons, or their brothers, or their brothers' sons or sisters' sons, or their women, or their slaves, or male attendants who lack vigour, or children who know naught of women's nakedness. And let them not stamp their feet so as to reveal what they hide of their adornment. And turn unto Allāh together, O believers, in order that ye may succeed. (Q. 24 : 30, 31)

Thus it was enjoined that one should not stare at another under sex impulse and keep one's eyes lowered while talking to another of a different sex ; and this injunction was obligatory on both men and women. Further, women were advised not to let the "treasures of the body" be exposed to the view of others. According to the Qur'ān, however, it is not necessary for a woman to remain confined within the four walls of her house, nor to cover her face or hands or those parts of the body which necessarily remain uncovered in normal daily activity or "are normally exposed to view".

The recompense for good living viz., happy life in heaven, is repeatedly promised both to man and woman.

> "I will not suffer the work of any worker among you to be lost whether male or female,
>
> The one of you being from the other". (Q. 3 : 194)
>
> "But whoso doth the things that are right, whether male or female, and he or she a believer,—these shall enter

Paradise, nor shall they be wronged the skin of a date stone". (Q. 4:123)

"To the faithful, both men and women, God promiseth gardens 'neath which the rivers flow, in which they shall abide, and goodly mansions in the gardens of Eden. But best of all will be God's good pleasure in them. This will be the great bliss." (Q. 9:73)

"Whoso doeth that which is right, whether male or female, if a believer, him will we surely quicken to a happy life, and recompence them with a reward meet for their best deeds". (Q. 16 : 99)

"Truly the men who resign themselves to God, and the women who resign themselves, and the believing men and the believing women, and the devout men and the devout women, the men of truth, and the women of truth, the patient men and the patient women, the humble men and the humble women, the men who give alms, and the women who give alms, the men who fast and the women who fast, the chaste men and the chaste women, and the men and the women who oft remember God: for them hath God prepared forgiveness and a rich recompense". (Q. 33:35)

JEHĀD

The term 'Jehād' bears a variety of cannotations in the Qur'ān. The ordinary sense of the term is "to try to set things right" or simply 'to exert' in a good cause.

The expression 'Jehād-fi-Sabilallah' meaning 'to exert in the way of Allāh' has been used very freely in the Qur'ān. In the initial stages of the Prophetic mission, adherents of the Prophet sought refuge in Ethiopia, in consequence of their persecution by the tribe of Quraish. The Qur'ān designated their action as 'Jehad of life and property in the way of Allāh'.

"Verily, they who have believed and fled their homes and spent their substance in the way of God, and they who have taken in the prophet and been helpful to him, shall be near of kin, the one to the other". (Q. 8:73)

"But as for those who have believed and fled their country, and fought in the way of God, and given the Prophet an

asylum, and been helpful to him, these are the faithful; Mercy is their due and a noble provision". (Q. 8:75)
"And they who have believed and fled their country since, and have worked hard at your side, these also are of you." (Q. 8:76)

This type of Jehād did not involve any use of arms. In fact, at this stage, permission to take up arms had not been, given. On the other hand, the injunction was not to retaliate, but to bear every ordeal with patience and, as far as possible, to return good for evil.

The Qur'ān indeed asked the Prophet to go on persuading strenuously in affection and goodwill not merely his opponents of Mecca but even those followers of his who were not wholely sincere in their profession or were hypocrites to follow the path of righteousness. Persuasion also was called 'Jehad' (Q. 9:73; 66:9).

In the face of these clear statements, Mawlavi Muhammad Ali in his Commentary of the Qur'ān says: "to give to the term 'Jehād' the meaning of 'to fight with arms' is to betray rank ignorance of the idiom and usage of the Arabic language".

The Qur'ān asks the Prophet: "Give not therefore to the unbelievers, but by means of the Qur'ān *strive* against them with a mighty striving" (Q. 25:54). Commenting on this verse, Mawlavi Muhammad Ali says: "It is clear from this verse what meaning the Qur'ān intends to give to the term 'Jehād'". It is a well-known fact that this verse was delivered in the Meccan period of the Prophet's mission when permission was not afforded to the Muslims to take up arms. The verse makes it clear that the highest form of Jehad or the greatest Jehad is to exert streneously in the cause of truth by the Quranic method of persuasion. In fact, the commentators like Baiḍawi, Abū Hyyān and others uphold the same interpretation. The Qur'ān has repeatedly called migration to another place or seeking refuge from persecution and protecting one's faith and patiently enduring the consquent suffering as a great Jehad (Q. 16:110). The Qur'ān calls the giving of anything in charity, the taking care of the indigent and the orphans, the offering of help to others, the enduring of suffering as Jehād-fī-sabilallāh. There is a well known saying of the Prophet in which he designates the control of one's anger, desires and passions as 'the Great Jehād'. It is the conquering of the self which in Arabic is called the Great Jehād or the Greatest Jehād.

Activities such as prayer, fasting and dispensing of charity are called Mujāhida, a term derived from the same root as that from which the term 'Jehād' is derived.

We may, with confidence, assert three things in respect of this term 'Jehād'.

1. Wherever this term has been used in the Qur'ān, it does not signify or imply the use of arms. In matters religious, it denotes 'a worthy striving'.
2. Nowhere in the Qur'ān is the term 'Jehād' used to denote *only* 'fighting with arms'.
3. There is no doubt that in particular situations, the Qur'ān gives permission to take up arms. But in the language used, the term 'Jehād' is not employed. On the other hand, the term used is 'Qital', 'to fight'.

On the subject of 'Jehād', the works that need to be consulted are 'Jehād' by Mawlavi Chirag Ali, and Al-jehād-fil-Islām by Mawlana Abul Kalam Azad.

THE LIFE HEREAFTER

The terms ''Āquibat' and 'Ākhirat' are used to denote the life after death, where one has to account for what one has done in his life here. The term ''Āqibat' is also used to denote the consequences of one's actions.

Jannath (Heaven) and Jehannam (Hell) are also freely used in the Qur'ān. Muslim scholars hold different views on whether 'the soul' assigned to hell is to dwell there eternaly or for a temporary period. But the greatest among them hold the view that the thought of eternity in hell is repugnant to the

Qur'ānic ideology. There are sayings of the Prophet which state "That a time would come when no human soul would remain in hell".

There are various verses in the Qur'ān which suggest that the visions of heaven and hell raised therein are merely figurative in import (Q. 16 : 24,25,26). Speaking of these verses Mawlavi Muhammad Ali says:

> "The parable likening a good word to a good tree follows immediately a description of the final abode of those who do good, which is repeatedly described in the Holy Qur'ān as being a Garden or Gardens wherein rivers flow. This gives us a clue to the real nature of Paradise. A good word is like a good tree which gives its fruit in every season, and therefore the fruits which a man will find in paradise, every ready and within his reach, are only the fruits of his own good deeds. The trees of paradise are in fact man's own good deeds, which have grown into trees, bearing a fruit which is an embodiment of the spiritual fruits of the good deeds of this life. It should also be noted that, as good deeds are likened to fruit-bearing trees, faith is likened to water repeatedly in the Holy Qur'ān, being the source of physical life. It is for this reason that, just as the righteous are always spoken of as being those who believe and do good, paradise is always described as being a Garden in which rivers flow, the rivers corresponding to faith and the trees of the Garden corresponding to the good which a man does."

In verse 15 of Chapter 47 it is pointed out that the picture given of Heaven with its running streams, its variety of fruits, and the picture of hell with its boiling water are metaphorical.

> "A parable which is promised to the God-fearing! Therein are rivers of water, which corrupt not: rivers of milk, whose taste changeth not: and rivers of wine, delicious to those who quaff it;
>
> "And rivers of honey clarified: and therein are all kinds of fruit for them from their Lord! Is this like the lot of those who must dwell for ever in the fire? And shall have draughts of boiling water forced on them which will rend their bowels assunder?" (Q. 47 : 16, 17)

Here and there, the suffering wrought by one's own self or as the result of one's deeds is called 'hell'. Likewise, the result of good deeds in life or the good things in life enjoyed by one's own exertion are styled 'Jannath' or heaven. There is a well-known saying of the Prophet in which he gives the name of Jannath to the rivers of Egypt, Iraq and Iran (Muslim. Vol. II. page 351).

Along with the term 'Jannath', the Qur'ān in several places, uses the term 'Hur'! The term is masculine in gender as against 'Hura', the feminine gender of it. The Qur'ān promises Jannath to men and women alike who have lived righteous lives. But the term Hur wherever used is not used in the sense of beings meant to pander to any human passions (Q. 44 : 54, 37 : 48, 56 : 36).

On a casual reading of the description of Hur in the Qur'ān, one may be inclined to take it as the picture of a woman. But in reality the referenec signifies the spiritual blessings following righteous life. Nowhere is it pointed out in the Qur'ān that the relations between man and woman in the life hereafter will be the same as subsist in this life. Spiritual blessings, whatever they are, are promised equally to both man and woman. But this, one may assert with definiteness, that the pleasures of heaven, as visualized, bear no resemblance whatsoever to the pleasures of the senses that one feels in this life. A saying of the Prophet runs: "God says: the good fruits that God has provided for his good servants are such as no eyes have rested on, nor any ears have ever heard of, nor any heart and mind have ever sensed" (Bukhari). One thing is clear from a careful reading of the Qur'ān that the references to Heaven and Hell therein are figurative in character and have nothing to do with the corporeal senses of pleasure and pain.

In Arabic 'Jannath' means a garden or a place of rest and 'Jehnnam' was the name given to a locality in Jerusalem where once fire worshippers used to live. Jehnnam has thus come to mean 'fire' or place of suffering 'Dozakh' is a Persian word and means exactly what the Sanskrit term 'Dukh' connotes. The Persian Firdos or Paradise in English or Pradesh in

Sanskrit are of the same root. Ancient Iranians used to call the gardens in the suburbs of their cities as Pradesh or 'Pardos' which ultimately have assumed the forms of 'Firdos' and 'Paradise'.

FURTHER VERSES.

How can ye withhold faith from God? Ye were dead and He gave you life; next He will cause you to die; next He will restore you to life: next shall ye return to Him! (Q. 2:26)

Verily God causeth the grain and the date stone to put forth. He bringeth forth the living from the dead, and the dead from the living! This is God! Why, then, are ye turned aside from Him? (Q. 6-95)

And He it is who hath given you life, then will cause you to die, then will give you life — of a truth man is ungrateful. (Q. 22:65)

O ye who believe! seek help with patience and with prayer, for God is with the patient.

And say not those who are slain on God's path that they are Dead; nay, they are Living! But ye understand not-

With somewhat of fear and hunger, and loss of wealth, and lives and fruits, will we surely test you: but bear good tidings to the patient,

Who when a mischance chanceth them, say, "Verily we are God's, and to Him shall we return:

On them shall be blessings from their Lord, and mercy; and these!—they are rightly guided. (Q. 2:148-152)

God is the friend of believers: He shall bring them out of darkness into light: (Q. 2:258)

Now hath a light and a clear Book come to you from God, by which God will guide him who shall follow after his good pleasure, to paths of peace, and will bring them out of the darkness to the light, by his will: and to the straight path will he guide them. (Q. 5:18)

He it is who hath sent down to thee "the Book". Some of its signs are of themselves perspicuous; — these are the basis of the Book — and others, are figurative. But they whose hearts are given to err, follow its figures, craving discord, craving an interpretation; yet none knoweth its interpretation but God, And the stable in knowledge say, "We believe in it: it is all from our Lord", But none will bear this in mind, save men endued with understanding. (Q. 3:5)

Verily God is not ashamed to set forth as well the instance of a gnat as of any nobler object: for as to those who have believed, they know it to be the truth from their Lord; but as to the unbelievers, they will say, "What meaneth God by this comparison?" Many will He mislead by such parables and many guide: but none will He mislead thereby except the wicked. (Q. 2:24)

Among the people of the Book are some, to one of whom if thou entrust a thousand dinars, he will restore them to thee: And there is of them to whom if thou entrust a dinar, he will not restore it to thee, unless thou be ever instant with him.

This because they say, "we are not bound to keep faith with the ignorant (Pagan) folk, and they utter a lie against God, and know they do so:"

But whoso is true to his engagement, and feareth God,—verily God loveth those that fear him. (Q. 3:68-70)

And repute not those slain on God's path to be dead.
Nay, alive with their Lord, are they richly sustained.
(Q. 3:163)

And the life of this world is but comfort of illusion.
(Q. 3:182)

Woe to every backbiter, defamer!
Who amasseth wealth and storeth it against the future!
He thinketh surely that his wealth shall be with him for ever.
Nay! for verily he shall be flung into the Crushing Fire;
And who shall teach thee what the Crushing Fire is?
It is God's kindled fire,
Which shall mount above the hearts;
It shall verily rise over them like a vault,
On outstretched columns. (Q. 104:1-9)

Say: Truly my Lord hath forbidden filthy actions whether open or secret, and iniquity, and unjust violence, and to associate with God that for which He hath sent down no warranty, and to speak of God that ye know not.
(Q. 7:32)

And commit not disorders on the earth after it hath been well ordered; and call on Him with fear and longing desire: Verily, the mercy of God is nigh unto the righteous.
(Q. 7:54)

This, because, God changeth not the favour with which he favoureth a people, so long as they change not what is in their hearts; and for that God Heareth, Knoweth.
(Q. 8:55)

Each hath a succession of angels before him and behind him, who watch over him by God's behest. Verily God will not change his gifts to men, till they change what is in themselves: and when God willeth evil unto men, there is none can turn it away, nor have they any protector beside Him. (Q. 13:12)

And never have we sent a warner to any city whose opulent men did not say, "In sooth we disbelieve your message."

And they said, "We are the more abundant in riches and in children, nor shall we be among the punished".

Say: Of a truth my Lord will be liberal or sparing in his supplies to whom he pleaseth: but the greater part of men acknowledge it not.

Neither by your riches nor by your children shall you bring yourselves into nearness with Us; (Q. 34:33-36)

Whoso will choose the harvest field of the life to come, to him will we give increase in this his harvest field: and whoso chooseth the harvest field of this life, thereof will we give him: but no portion shall there be for him in the life to come. (Q. 42:19)

But if they turn aside from thee, yet we have not sent thee to be their guardian. 'Tis thine but to preach.
(Q. 42:47)

Know ye that this world's life is only a sport, and pastime, and show, and a cause of vainglory among you! And the multiplying of riches and children is like the plants which spring up after rain — Their growth rejoiceth the husband-man; then they wither away, and thou seest them all yellow; then they become stubble. And in the next life is a severe chastisement. (Q. 57:19)

O ye who believe! Verily, in your wives and your children ye have an enemy: wherefore beware of them. But if ye pass it over and pardon, and are lenient, then God too is Lenient, Merciful.

Your wealth and your children are only a source of trial! but God! with Him is the great recompense.
(Q. 64 : 14-15)

Then verily along with trouble cometh ease.
Verily along with trouble cometh ease. (Q. 94 : 5-6)

O ye who believe! fear God and believe in his apostle: two portions of his mercy will He give you. He will bestow on you light to walk in, and He will forgive you: for God is Forgiving, Merciful. (Q. 57 : 28)

Happy he who is purified
And who remembereth the name of his Lord and prayeth.
But ye prefer this present life,
Though the life to come is better and more enduring.
This truly is in the books of old,
The books of Abraham and Moses. (Q. 87 : 14-18)

Oh, thou soul which art at rest,
Return to they Lord, pleased, and pleasing him:
Enter thou among my servants,
And enter thou my Paradise. (Q. 89 : 27-30)

By the Sun and his noonday brightness!
By the Moon when she followeth him!
By the Day when it revealeth his glory!
By the Night when it enshroudeth him;
By the Heaven and Him who built it!
By the Earth and Him who spread it forth!
By a Soul and Him who balanced it
And breathed into it its wickedness and its piety,
Blessed now is he who hath kept it pure,
And undone is he who hath corrupted it! (Q. 91 : 1-10)

ESSENCE OF THE QUR'ĀN

In conclusion, we propose to summarise very briefly the basic principles of Islam and its fundamental teaching. The following are its basic principles:

(1) God is one. He has no form and none is like Him. He is the Lord of all the worlds, and requites everyone for what one does. To him alone one must offer wor hip and to none else.

(2) All mankind are servants of God, and every human being is a brother unto every other. Superiority of one over another lies in the character of the good that one does and the manner in which one shuns evil.

(3) All great religions are inspired by God. The founder of each has received his light from this One common Source. For that reason, all religions are at the base but one and the same.

(4) Customs, manners, and modes of worship differ from religion to religion as warranted by circumstance under which each was delivered. But there is no difference between them in basic principles. Disputes arise where people side-track these basic principles and lay undue stress on customs, manners and modes of worship.

(5) Righteousness does not lie in turning to East or West in prayer. It lies in sincere belief in one God of all creation, and in righteous living. The Qur'ān

enjoins both prayer and fasting; but it has not laid down any specific method for prayer, nor laid down any specific regulations for fasting. (The details are, however, furnished by the traditions of the Prophet:- Translator). The Qur'ān points the purposes underlying them, viz. that "one should avoid evil, and do good." He who believes in God and works righteously, whatever the religion that he may follow, asserts the Qur'ān, "no fear shall come upon him, nor shall he grieve."

(6) Whenever a community or people turned away from the basic principles of religion, God raised among them a prophet or a messenger of truth from Him to re-establish the true religion among them, or al-Din, in order that they might come back to the right path. Such prophets have arisen in all communities and in all countries, each delivering the message in his own language.

(7) To discriminate between one prophet and another, or to accept some and reject the other is sin.

(8) The Qur'ān confirms the message embodied in all scriptures delivered before it and styles Prophet Muhammad as the Seal of all prophets, since he has endorsed whatever that had been delivered by the prophets gone before Him.

(9) Even like the Gītā, the Qur'ān permits its followers, under certain conditions, to take up arms in the defence of their faith. Both ask them to desist from fighting, if the enemy seeks peace. There is no compulsion in religion. That is a basic principle of the Qur'ān. In every field of activity, the clear Qur'ānic direction is: "It is always good for man to forgive the wrongs inflicted on him by others and endure them with patience and return good for evil", for "God is gracious and forgives all". Verily, "God loves those only who do good to others."

The Qur'ān lays its special emphasis on two things. One is faith: the other is good deeds or righteous activity. In respect of the former, one should believe in One God and in all the scriptures inspired by him and all the prophets raised among all the peoples and in the good forces of life and finally in the life after death. In respect of the other, one should keep his desires under proper control and do good to others.

The truth is that the basic principles of the Qur'ān, even as of other great scriptures, constitute a universal message for all mankind and point clearly to every earnest mind the way to religious and spiritual progress. If we approach the Qur'ān with sincerity and love, we are bound to realise that it offers to us that universal humanism which is the essence of all religions, called by the Hindu Sants "Prem Dharam" and by the Muslim Sufis "Madhhab-i-'Ishq", the Religion of Love."

INDEX

Names and Books

CORRIGENDA

READ	CORRECT	FOR	INCORRECT	PAGE	LINE
,,	there		thre	12	4
,,	Weigh		weight	22	26
,,	one		once	40	6
delete			with	46	24
Read	discord		discard	48	25
,,	as		a	57	27
,,	purpose		purfose	64	9
,,	then		than	77	13
,,	manifest		munifest	81	7
,,	imperilled		imprelled	86	15
,,	There		Tnere	93	8
,,	degraded		degarded	96	5
,,	The		Thee	107	37
,,	We		Whe	109	15
,,	to		wto	123	31
,,	firmly		flrmly	124	16
,,	prosper		proposer	125	28
,,	him		whim	126	26
,,	weigh		weight	127	9
,,	then		than	128	33
,,	unclean		unclelan	133	32
,,	Thy		They	143	19